To Pam and Jeremy:
I hope you enjoy these essays
and that love's magic brings you
much happiness

Warm Regards,
Janice [illegible]
.2001.

With a Foreword by John M. Gottman

Janice R. Levine *and* Howard J. Markman, Editors

JOSSEY-BASS
A Wiley Company
San Francisco

Jossey-Bass books and products are available through most bookstores. To contact Jossey-Bass directly, call (888) 378-2537, fax to (800) 605-2665, or visit our website at www.josseybass.com.

Substantial discounts on bulk quantities of Jossey-Bass books are available to corporations, professional associations, and other organizations. For details and discount information, contact the special sales department at Jossey-Bass.

Printed in the United States of America.
Book design by Claudia Smelser.

Library of Congress Cataloging-in-Publication Data

Why do fools fall in love? : experiencing the magic, mystery, and meaning of successful relationships / Janice R. Levine and Howard S. Markman, eds.; with a foreword by John M. Gottman—1st ed.

p. cm.

Includes bibliographical references.

ISBN 0-7879-5384-9 (alk. paper)

1. Love. 2. Man-woman relationships. I. Levine, Janice R. (Janice Ruth), date. II. Markman, Howard, date. III. Title.

BF575.L8 W54 2000

152.4'1—dc21 00-011115

FIRST EDITION

HB Printing 10 9 8 7 6 5 4 3 2 1

Contents

Foreword

Jan Levine and Howard Markman asked me what percentage of marital success is chemistry and what percentage is social skill. My response was that it is mostly chemistry. What I meant was that it isn't possible to be married to just anyone, but what matters most is the matching.

I believe there's a wide range of people with whom it might be possible for each of us to have a successful marriage. In all of these cases there is a lock-in-key fit that works. The theory of corrective social skills suggests that one could make marriage work by doing the right thing at the right time. I don't believe that, because nothing works unless it is genuine, unless it comes from the heart, unless it really has that special key.

For example, does his face naturally brighten when she walks into a room? When he reads something interesting, is he thinking, "I'd like to get her view on this"? Or are all these things an afterthought—an applied social skill? When we study couples who truly "master" marriage, we notice that, for example, her sense of humor is delightful to him and eases his heart, even though they're discussing a difficult, long-standing issue. To another man she might seem irritating.

None of this works unless it is genuine. His interest in her and the effect of her anger or humor on his heart rate and endocrine secretions are all determined by the fit between them, that is, by the chemistry. This volume poses the central question, What is this chemistry, and how do you get it? Or if you have it, how do you keep it and nourish it?

It is possible to describe what the masters of marriage do when they are together in various important contexts, compared to the disasters of marriage. Compared to the disasters, the masters

- Are interested in one another (they make maps of their partner's inner psychological world)
- Display fondness and admiration, and maintain affection and respect
- Are clear (and at times playful) in making bids for emotional connection in non-conflict situations, which encourages their partners to turn toward them instead of away from or against them
- Have generally positive sentiments that override momentary irritability, instead of being in a state where generally negative sentiments override momentary positivity
- Know how to dialogue and cope with their perpetual, unsolvable problems (which are 69 percent of all marital problems) instead of being either in attack-defend mode or emotionally disengaged on these issues
- Have a gentle approach to their issues (they soften the way they raise the issue; they accept influence from one another, and they repair and de-escalate conflict to create physiological soothing in themselves and in their partner)

- Can recover from arguments, understand one another's reality of the fight, understand how the argument became painful, and repair the relationship by improving their next conversation on the issue
- Have been able to honor one another's life dreams
- Have been able to create a system of shared meaning through rituals of connection, shared meaning for important roles, shared values and goals, and narratives about their history and purpose
- Have been able to create community as a context within which this relationship operates and is supported

I believe we'll eventually find ways to help about 70 percent of the people who wish to salvage their ailing relationships make clinically significant improvements. Some of these couples were probably mismatched in the first place, but their mismatches will turn into perpetual issues that they can cope with. The other 30 percent are fatally mismatched.

Some of the most difficult mismatches we have identified so far are in preferred influence style and people's feelings about fundamental emotions (for example, anger, sadness, fear, affection, and pride) and in the importance of leading an emotional life (introspection and expression). Those two are the hardest mismatches to cope with for couples, and they are highly predictive of divorce. There are probably others we haven't studied yet, such as mismatches in playfulness, mismatches in style of conversation, mismatches in sense of humor, mismatches in sexual play. These mismatches either lead to perpetual problems that the couple can live with and dialogue about, or they trigger enduring vulnerabilities that leave one or both feeling fundamentally rejected, unappreciated, and unloved.

The most important mismatch, however, is existential. Can people support one another in their life dreams? Can they develop a common sense of purpose, value, and mission that makes this brief journey of ours through life mean something? Can they really create, in this family, a new culture (and culture is all about meaning) that works? Marital therapy has failed in large measure because it hasn't examined the existential meaning of the most gridlocked issues—what we call the dream within the conflict.

The essays in this volume are important for defining this dream, this chemistry. In my opinion the chemistry is not love; nor is it having fallen or not having fallen in love; nor is it passion. It is a kind of surrender—a surrender to one's partner's charm and power, a surrender whose presence or absence we can easily measure but cannot contrive any more than we can contrive a genuine laugh or an orgasm. That surrender is the magic; it is the "falling" part of falling in love.

John M. Gottman
James Mifflin Professor of Psychology
University of Washington, Seattle

Preface

Dear Readers:

We have both spent our professional lives studying how relationships work and, like most people, are not strangers to some painful lessons about love and life. We say *most people* because we know that relationships are never easy and that love, although certainly necessary, is never sufficient to withstand all of what life affords.

Over the years we've come to believe that there may indeed be a kind of science to *staying* in love but that this only works if a person has already *fallen* in love. We've also learned, however, that love cannot be willed or designed. Since without this capricious emotion relationships cannot survive, we thought it important to understand love's secrets.

Three years ago at the SmartMarriages conference where we were both presenting, we ran into John Gottman, one of the eminent researchers in the field of relationship studies. We asked him a simple but fateful question: "What percentage of happy and successful relationships do you think is due to the person we choose versus the skills we have?"

His answer was as startling as it was intuitively true: "Ninety-nine percent," he said without hesitation, "is due to the person we choose." So . . . all of our professional work targets 1 percent of the variance and 99 percent is left to Cupid?

Since then we have had countless conversations about the nature of love, which is how this book was ultimately inspired. We decided that without a better understanding of love's dimensions, our work (not to mention our lives) would be incomplete. So we decided to probe the minds of the experts in an effort to come up with some answers.

To be sure, what we discovered is that there are as many insights into love's nature as there are thinkers and lovers. Indeed, there are no fixed answers; what's true for one is not true for all. But we can tell you some things that we *have* learned about the magic, mystery, and meaning of successful relationships.

The *magic,* we believe, is in the fall. It's that *je ne sais quoi* of chemistry to which we can only surrender. Why we fall in love with someone—and become altered by the process—is probably some combination of serendipity, biochemistry, and divinity. Beyond that, we cannot know.

Mystery is about the pull of the unknown. It's about the infinite potential for discovery between two individuals in love. Mystery feeds desire. This is the energy that draws—and keeps—two people together in pursuit of a meaningful existence.

It is in the *meaning,* however, that our lives achieve purpose. And meaning is revealed through this very process of committing to a lifetime of mutual discovery with a beloved other.

What we have here is just a beginning. But even though love may often elude our attempts to know it, we come away from this project convinced more than ever that it is our capacity to love that defines our essential humanity and bids us to grow. Besides, nothing feels better! Whatever it takes to find our way there, we think the journey is well worth taking.

Janice R. Levine ❧ *Howard J. Markman*

To Brian,

who turned reality into dreams.

—J.R.L.

To my loving and supportive parents,

Claire and Arnold,

for having had the courage to weather the storms
and creating a marriage full of fun, friendship, and happiness.

—H.J.M.

Acknowledgments

We have many people to thank for helping us make this book a reality. There are those who helped with the nuts and bolts of its execution and those who helped in perhaps less tangible but more meaningful ways. We first want to acknowledge and thank our own support network.

Above all, I (Jan) want to thank my children, Brennan and Sarah, for their love, encouragement, and pride in me. These two souls required, just by their beings, that I abandon any pre-set notions of love in favor of the promise that comes only from listening with an open heart. Lesson learned: love is natural and limitless if we don't mess with it. Dad, Esther, and Fred: you saw and loved, straight and simple. Thank you. I needed that. Mom, Barb, and Brian: would that it always *were* that simple! Without your love and tenacity I would never have asked the questions, never stretched and grown to know love's deeper truths. Karen, you've been a constant presence in my heart and a pulse behind this book. Love is a magical and healing force. Brian, your wonderful, unswerving, authentic self has made sharing life with you a blessing and an odyssey I'd never want to live without. Thank you for your unqualified love and support in every crazy thing I undertake.

Then there are those who could have chosen otherwise but didn't—who love me for free. Love and thanks, always, to my wonderful and devoted friends: Sandy, Jesse, Ronnie, Amy, Nancy, Joanie, Dewie, Abbe, Kim, Rami, and Scott. You are my mainstays. My life is blessed by your friendship. Howie, thank you for sharing this adventure with me and for being the best partner and friend I could have hoped for. Your heart is always in the right place.

I (Howard) would like to thank my two wonderful children, Mat and Leah, who are the jewels of my life and have helped me know the true meaning of love. I would like to thank the great friends who have shared meaningful moments of my life over the years: Mark, Scott, Art, Tony, George, Mike, David, Norm, Elsbeth, and Mitch. Janine, you are a special friend and a magical spirit. Barry, you are a special brother who is also a great friend and teammate. Jan, you are a poet as well as my partner on this project. Beauty and magic equally touch your soul and your writing. Thanks for everything!

Both of us want to offer special thanks to the people who helped with this project in ways large and small: Alan Rinzler, our editor at Jossey-Bass, for his vision, wisdom, inspiration, and support, and for sticking it out with us even when we faltered; Amy Scott for helping with all the details and for never being too bothered by our naïve questions; Ruthie Rivin—you were heaven sent. Many thanks for pulling out the stops and helping us when no one else in the industry would. Lenore Levine: as promised, thank you for your research help. How were we to know that he'd not go with funny! We're grateful to University of Denver students

Kimberly Siwiec, Lindsay Fiedelman, and Jennifer Bell for their helpful and thorough research on celebrity quotes. Diane Sollee, as always, thank you for helping us network with many of our esteemed contributors. Finally, a special thanks goes to John Gottman, not only for his beautiful Foreword but for so honestly answering the auspicious question that helped inspire this book.

To all of our wonderful contributors: Wow! Our dream came true with each of you. What a privilege it's been to read your ideas and to learn things we might never have known without access to your insights and wisdom. Each of you has been a delight to know and work with, and it goes without saying that your beautiful pearls have made this book all that it is. Thank you for your generous spirit. Let's hope we make a difference.

—J.R.L.
—H.J.M.

Introduction

"You're not sick, you're just in love," explains Irving Berlin. "Lord, what fools we mortals be," decides Shakespeare's Puck. Are we fools to want to fall in love or just fools for having fallen? Or is it perhaps not foolish at all to fall in love? We may never fully understand what accounts for this universal and elusive condition, but like moths to a flame, we can be certain that we will fall again, and again, and again.

Why are we so compelled to fall in love? What is this mysterious life force that most of us desire, even knowing full well the pain, loss, fear, and angst that often accompany it? How do we explain an energy so subjective that it strikes only the eyes of the beholders, so transformative that mind and body have no choice but to surrender, so powerful that it can bind two people together for a lifetime, and so magical that it defies rational explanation? How, we wonder, are we to understand the nature of this tender beast that breathes life into our most cherished relationships?

Social scientists know well that our survival and cultural livelihood depend on understanding the kinds of feelings and behaviors that allow relationships to thrive. Indeed, we have amassed a wealth of data that can prescribe what to do more of and less of, that suggest verbal formulas for better communication, and that identify actual mathematical ratios of good-to-bad interactions that allow us to predict who will stay happily married. Curiously, however, these scientific inquiries tend to avoid studying the one, powerfully invisible, central phenomenon without which none of the other variables hold meaning or utility: *love.*

And with good reason. Love, as we all know, is neither a singular nor an objective phenomenon, and as such it defies our ability to define or study it precisely. To try to do so would be to undermine love's more magical and mysterious qualities—the very qualities our book wishes to explore. Yet perhaps if we *could* understand love's method, that flame we seek could be fanned into warmth and longevity rather than threaten to burn us—and then burn out.

Hoping to learn more about how love fuels and sustains relationships, we invited thirty of our most thoughtful colleagues and relationship experts to share their personal views about the nature of love. We wanted to probe the minds of these colleagues—the various authors, academics, mediators, counselors, marriage therapists, and educators who have impressed us over the years with their wisdom and ability to express a deeper meaning beyond mere technique or problem solving. Specifically, we invited them to write an essay that would go beyond the more coolly mechanical aspects of this field to create a deeper, more complete vision of what constitutes truly happy long-term relationships—in one thousand words or less!

The responses were positively inspiring. These essays stretch beyond the limits of scientific research to reveal a kind of magic that lives between lovers. The authors describe an energy so basic to intimate relationships that without it none of the skills we teach could take hold.

For example, Steven Pinker suggests that we must rely on an irrational, self-negating emotion to sustain marriage. Henry Grunebaum thinks love is wise. Dee Watts-Jones sees love as a process of "opening," Janice Levine as one of "beholding." Wayne and Mary Sotile believe love is about heroism. Pat Love and Sunny Shulkin suggest that we are rendered virtually helpless when struck by Cupid's chemical cocktail. Frank Pittman and Jessica Bethoney caution us that to follow our passion is a death wish, whereas Peggy and James Vaughan suggest that we haven't lived fully unless we risk going for "the Full Monty." For Shirley Glass, "The Harder We Fall, the Farther We Fall." Charlie Verge argues that love and devotion can bring us to the highest level of spiritual awakening. Harville Hendrix unravels love's underlying psychological knot, but Peter Fraenkel believes that, quite simply, we get a kick out of the people we love. Stephen Gilligan thinks we die multiple deaths in marriage for the same reason that James Hollis directs us to relinquish our search for a Magical Other—to grow up. Steven Stosny welcomes the mirror that marriage affords, yet Amy Gerson cautions us against seeking our own "psychological mirage" in soul mates. Karen Blaisure pinpoints the power of gratitude, Rita DeMaria the bond, Scott Stanley the sacrifice. And these represent but a sampling.

To further tantalize you, a variety of short quotes and exercises are sprinkled in the margins alongside each essay. These sidebars, drawn from a variety of sources, including the authors themselves, poets, and even some well-known celebrities, highlight each essay's key ideas and provide a kind of sneak preview into what the essay is about.

Even though each essay is unique, we have arranged the collection into four broad subsections or themes. The first section looks at love's *Magic.* There we explore how love miraculously transforms us. These authors consider whether love's magic is to be trusted and cherished above all else or instead renders us chemically altered, "foolish mortals" in pursuit of a mere fantasy. We then consider love's *Meaning,* from the broadest personal and spiritual perspective to love's more limited and specific dimensions. In *Marriage* we are given a view into the interiors of various long-term relationships and discover what successful marriages entail. Finally, the section on *Mastery* clarifies many of love's mysteries and helps us learn important lessons about how to love well.

We present this unabridged volume of essays about love with no commentary and no attempt to propose a unifying theory or come to any final conclusions. Instead we offer an array of perspectives from which we hope you will find something meaningful to you, as well as a key to unlocking your own capacity to love. We may agree or disagree with what these authors have to say but, like you, we are all students, open to learning, and amazed at the range of insights from which we can choose. Read this book as if each sidebar were a sweet flirtation, each essay a warm embrace. We hope you enjoy the magic within.

MAGIC

Behold: The Power of Love

Janice R. Levine

To love is to behold—to fall fully open to the amazing wonders of another human soul. There is no magic more beautiful and powerful than the energy that transforms us in the presence of a beloved other. Is it magic or divinity? I'm convinced it must be divine. How else could the survival of our species be so elegantly ensured?

Just consider love's many dimensions. On a biological level, the very survival of our species depends on love. This single, powerful energy is at the heart of every basic need, from nurturance and protection through procreation. Biologists maintain that love is not only what defines us humanly but that it is the very agent of both our individual growth and collective evolution. Imagine: our cellular structures and neural pathways are literally altered through the agency of love, as we open ourselves to receive another human environment into our own. Amazing!

On a social level, people who love and feel emotionally connected to others actually live longer and are more resilient to despair and disease than those who are alone or detached. Love somehow fortifies our immune systems, helps our bodies heal, and inoculates us against disease.

On an individual level, love can inspire us to grow beyond ourselves. Miraculously, love holds the potential to heal emotional wounds and move us beyond our fears and limitations. It opens us to look through eyes of wonder or see through the eyes of another soul.

On a spiritual level, love enables us to transcend our temporal and material world. It is as if, in our last moments, the meaning of life becomes suddenly clear: loving and feeling loved is the energy that drives everything else and that links us to the divine.

What *is* this elusive phenomenon that defies definition but that we could not endure without? I'm drawn to the words of the Buddhist monk, Thich Nhat Hanh: "To love means to listen," he teaches. "The capacity of listening to ourselves is the foundation of the capacity of listening to others." This capacity to truly *listen*—to perceive and experience another human being wholly—comes exclusively through the act of loving. It is the power to behold. And it begins with learning to behold and accept ourselves.

In my experience working with couples, I know this to be true.

Kelsey Grammer and Camille Donatacci

KELSEY: She listens to me. She offers kindness without my asking for it. There's a line I love: "living in the country of consideration." She is a considerate human being, and that's really important. I've never had that before. I'm glad I've got it now.

—*Redbook,* February 1999

The more I listen, the more I hear this basic need expressed: "Know me. Understand me. Respect my differences and accept my weaknesses. Love who I am, not who you need me to be. If I can feel this from you, then I will feel safe and free to give you all that I have to give."

Behold me—is at once a primary need and the highest expression of love. To love someone freely and without design allows you to see into their true nature and internal goodness. When this happens—when couples risk receiving each other "as is"—grace begins. The fight to defend who they are evaporates. Kindness becomes contagious, and being gracious supplants being right. Forgiveness becomes a gift to the relationship rather than a begrudging act of sacrifice. To feel loved and known releases our highest potential.

Love passes through many phases and by definition is never perfect. Or I should say, love becomes perfect only when we abandon the pursuit of perfection and instead embrace the beauty in our human flaws. This is the wonderful secret they never advertise: that happiness doesn't come from being or creating the perfect person. It comes from discovering the intrinsic perfection when you're with the person you love. We may never understand what draws any two human souls together, but we know this to be true:

something magical occurs between two people when they fall in love. It creates a force field so strong and persistent that life's greatest struggles and tragedies—even wars—have been surmounted when fueled by love's energy and promise alone. I wish I could tell you how this happens. I only know that love is hatched and not designed and that, when it happens, the love of another can engender the strength necessary to survive whatever challenges a lifetime presents.

But finding love is even less about finding the right person than it is about *being* the right person: it's about being someone who can replace the misdirected need to control or possess with the safety and serenity found in loving for its own sake. It's about being willing to behold the delightful "who" rather than the coveted "what." And then, miraculously, it's about discovering the capacity to surrender. Letting go allows us to let in. When we surrender to the vast promise of truly loving another, our lives achieve meaning and direction. We open ourselves to the dual possibilities of growth (being changed by another) and true internal peace (accepting our human flaws). And with surrender we open ourselves to a kind of passion that results only from having achieved a trusting sense of abandon.

With surrender we open ourselves to a kind of passion that results only from having achieved a trusting sense of abandon.

I was once a professional violinist. I've played on many violins, and they all respond differently. The key, I've discovered, to releasing an instrument's most beautiful sound is to know it so well, so intrinsically, that you simply understand what it responds to and what it doesn't: which strings need tenderness and which withstand force; how fast or hard to draw the bow; how to release a whisper and how to unleash passion. How one violin responds won't necessarily be like any other. Each has its own personality, and all your willpower or finesse can't convince it otherwise. The secret, I've discovered, is to work *with* rather than *against* the limits of your instrument and not try to force the music out of it. Only then will it give forth its most glorious song.

People respond the same way. Their beauty needs to be released, not extracted, and the only way to know how your lover responds is to listen carefully and behold their true nature. Love is the agency that allows us to do just that—to see into the interiors of our beloved and to cherish rather than judge what we observe. Love enables us to see past our own eyes, know past our own experiences, and disinhabit our bodies and minds in order to bear witness to the beauty of another human soul. Only with loving eyes can you truly see what your partner needs and responds to and thus become less likely to create obstacles for them to surmount in response to you.

Invite them to love you by making it easy. Release them from their defenses; know them so well that you understand how to dissolve fear, anger, and pride in your presence. Love with abandon and generosity, and then behold the power of love.

Fool's Love

Patricia Love

Why do fools fall in love? It's simple: because it feels good and they don't know any better. Falling in love is a no-brainer. We did it as adolescents; how sophisticated can it be? Staying in love, well, that's another matter. A fool in the throes of infatuation is doing nothing but following the call of the wild, which mandates us to meet, mate, procreate, and produce healthy offspring. Genes that control the immune system and push us toward mates with a different genetic structure from our own basically orchestrate this phenomenon of falling in love. That is, we are instinctively programmed to be physically attracted to a person whose DNA, in combination with ours, will produce virile descendants.

Although quite magnificent, this ubiquitous occurrence we have elevated to mystical heights actually has more to do with the divine order of the universe than whether a particular person is a suitable life mate. In fact, you can be highly attracted to someone who is impossible for you to live with. Attraction, as well as infatuation, has more to do with genes than gentility.

Falling in love is a no-brainer. We did it as adolescents; how sophisticated can it be?

Because Mother Nature knows that mating with someone whose DNA is similar (like a sibling or cousin) can produce less healthy offspring, she has designed you to be attracted to individuals who are genetically dissimilar. This attraction will occur whether you are committed or not, or whether you are happily or unhappily married. If you meet a DNA match, you will feel chemistry between you. What you do about that is up to you, and it will determine whether the fool is to be, or not to be.

Even though it's possible to be sexual with just about anybody, Nature has set it up so that most people are only inclined to have sex with individuals they find attractive. When you encounter a biological match, the pleasure centers in the brain are activated and produce a sense of delight. This causes you to move closer, at which point your pupils dilate and a small increase in the secretion of tear ducts causes your eyes to glisten, producing a "look of love" that is highly engaging.

If you meet a DNA match you will feel chemistry between you. What you do about that is up to you, and it will determine whether the fool is to be, or not to be.

With subsequent contact, feelings become more intense. Dopamine is released, producing a rush of pleasure; norepinephrine stimulates the production of adrenaline ("Be still my heart."); phenylethylamine (PEA) creates a feeling of euphoria.[1] But, this is just the beginning.

Under the influence of nature's "Love Potion #9," you go into a heightened state of alertness, notice every detail of the love object, and make special note of any sign of reciprocal interest. You develop a remarkable ability to emphasize what is truly admirable and avoid dwelling on any negative aspect. In the unlikely event of receiving negative information, you immediately respond with compassion and render it into another positive attribute (for example, "I love you for being honest about your cocaine habit."). During this time you can thrive on little sleep and tiny morsels of food. You are, after all, living on love and have never felt better. But there's still more.

During this time you can thrive on little sleep and tiny morsels of food. You are, after all, living on love and have never felt better.

In addition to giving you great pleasure, dopamine (a primary ingredient in the love cocktail) calls you to action. This marks the beginning of a long series of foolish acts, which can include anything from ignoring responsibilities (not to mention reality) to writing bad poetry. As if creating a state of bliss were not enough, PEA lowers all your defenses. It transforms a normally tight-lipped person into a blabbermouth, a non-toucher into a toucher, and a cold fish into a hot tamale. To keep up your energy, norepinephrine is released to supply the jet fuel for your rocket booster. At this point you and your lover hold on tight for the ride of your life.

Now you might be thinking, "Hey, this is what happened to me, and I've been happily married for twenty-nine years. Are you saying I've been foolish?" No. The wise and foolish alike go through this infatuation process when initially encountering a genetic match. But the wise know the difference between raw chemistry and true compatibility. If you've managed to create a loving, respectful relationship, you're not the fool in question. You were lucky enough to have been imprinted with a healthy image of love or somehow managed to get a partner who treats you well and meets your expectations. Not all of us have been this fortunate.

Regardless of what P. T. Barnum said, fools aren't born. They're created. Individuals learn to be foolish about love through prior experiences. Early in life, through interacting with the people who raised and influenced us, we formed a perception of love as well as a love partner. Young children perceive their family's values and habits as love, no matter how they are treated.[2] This means that if you grew up with your caregivers being warm and attentive, this is what you will expect from love, as well as from a partner. However, if you grew up with neglect, then being ignored by a partner not only feels familiar but it feels like love. (Harville Hendrix and Helen Hunt Hendrix popularized this phenomenon in their Imago theory and best-selling book, *Getting the Love You Want*.[3])

Fools aren't born. They're created. Individuals learn to be foolish about love through prior experiences.

Because of this early imprinting, you can foolishly be attracted to someone who treats you badly. And furthermore, if you are wired to expect love to be distant and cold, you will not be attracted to someone who is available and warm. Even though there may be initial chemistry because this person is a biological match, if he or she doesn't fit your image of love—foolish though it might be—you won't feel as though you are "in love." Consequently, some of us have to consciously change our image of love to "foolproof" our relationships.

Sadly, in the Western culture, we tend to equate *falling in love* with *being in love.* This is unfortunate because infatuation is a stage that ultimately passes. Scientific evidence has shown that within two years a natural state of neutrality sets in between two people in love. At this point, you must rely on your relational skills to keep love alive.

Thankfully, these skills are simple to learn. Research-based information is readily available. Love may be blind, especially in its earliest stages, but by opening your eyes and ears through discovery you can achieve deep and enduring love. Explore individual needs and expectations—and place priority on the relationship—to generate energy between you. Knowing that lows are normal will cast away fear and offer valuable lessons you can use to strengthen commitment. Authentic connection is the ultimate destination of a satisfied heart.[4]

Fortunately, it is never too late to learn. At any point in life you can exchange fool's love for true, everlasting love.

NOTES

1. Liebowitz, M. R. *The Chemistry of Love.* Boston: Little, Brown, 1983.
2. Hellinger, B. *Love's Hidden Symmetry.* Phoenix: Zeig, Tucker, 1998.
3. Hendrix, H. *Getting the Love You Want.* New York: Henry Holt, 1988.
4. Love, P. *The Satisfied Heart.* New York: Simon & Schuster, 2001.

The Myth of Passion

Jessica Bethoney

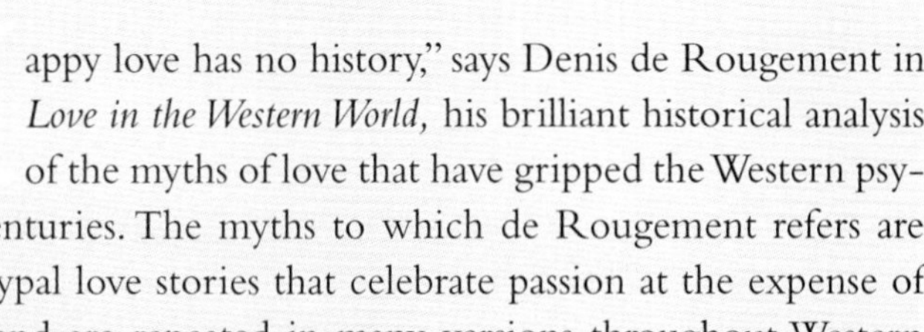

Happy love has no history," says Denis de Rougement in *Love in the Western World,* his brilliant historical analysis of the myths of love that have gripped the Western psyche for centuries. The myths to which de Rougement refers are the archetypal love stories that celebrate passion at the expense of marriage and are repeated in many versions throughout Western literature.

These myths are not mere fictions but are powerful narratives that symbolically describe the innermost longings of the human spirit. Many such myths, such as that of a lost Golden Age, exist in a multitude of diverse cultures. The myth of passion, however, is a

Western creation and one that permeates our culture and shapes the pattern of male-female relationships.

The love stories that speak to us from centuries past are tales of passion—not tales of happy, successful marriages. And passion by its very nature means suffering. Once ignited, passion requires obstacles to fan its flames. Lovers must be separated by societal constrictions, and their often illicit love can only be fully consummated in their death, such as happens in the story of Romeo and Juliet.

What are these stories telling us by making death passion's ultimate resolution? Why is passion not compatible with marriage? What is the nature of this yearning for union that can unleash the forces of destruction?

Passion by its very nature means suffering.

We may find these answers in a brief examination of one of the oldest and greatest tales of illicit love—the twelfth-century romance of Tristan and Iseult. Like its more familiar counterpart, the story of King Arthur, Lancelot, and Guenivere, Tristan and Iseult is the story of courtly love in which a knight betrays his king by having an adulterous relationship with the queen.

As the story unfolds, Tristan is on a mission to bring the golden-haired princess Iseult from her land to that of King Mark. During the boat trip, Iseult's maid mistakenly gives Tristan and Iseult wine laced with a love potion intended for Iseult and King Mark. As passion suddenly overwhelms Tristan and Iseult, they become its unwitting and unwilling prisoners. Their passion is literally and metaphorically a drug-induced state that is maintained only by the continual dose of suffering that separation causes the lovers.

When Tristan and Iseult's adultery is discovered, they flee to the forest, and after several years the effect of the love potion wanes. It is then that Tristan and Iseult discover a shocking truth. They were in love with love, not with each other! They decide to separate, only to pine for each other yet again. Their mutual suffering eventually ends as they join together in death.

Although eight centuries have passed since the creation of this tale, its vision of the human dilemma continues to resonate for us. It speaks to us not only of the potentially destructive nature of sexual passion but of the yearning for complete merger with another person, which, alas, cannot be achieved.

Although sexual passion can merely be the product of biological urges needing satisfaction, it can also be a manifestation of deeper psychic forces. It can propel us toward the person who we think will be our soul's companion—the person who will heal our psychological wounds or help us overcome our existential loneliness.

The story of Tristan and Iseult tells us first of all that passion can alter our state of mind so that we can be "in love" with a person we neither really know nor necessarily like. Second, the drama tells us that the heightened state of passionate love cannot be sustained in marriage. And third, although we certainly can have a deep connection on many levels with our partner, a total merger would mean the loss of our individual selves.

In a sense, true marriage can begin only when passion wanes. When we first begin a passionate relationship, we experience a so-called honeymoon period, during which we feel we have found the ideal lover. There is, however, a filter through which we behold this perfection—that of our own needs and desires. We may expect our partner to play a role in our emotional drama—perhaps that of the nurturing parent who will heal our childhood wounds or that of the soul mate who will end our loneliness. This projection of our own psyche not only colors our perception of our partner but may even prevent us from really knowing who that person is. When our partner does not live up to expectations or does not play his or her assigned role, the bubble of our passion bursts.

At this juncture, when we are forced to acknowledge our partner's separateness and individuality, we may choose either to dissolve the union or begin the process of discovery, acceptance, and appreciation of our partner's uniqueness. In order to do this, however, we must first come to terms with our own psychological and spiritual issues. We need to be comfortable with our own internal self-image and not dependent on the image of ourselves as reflected in the eyes of our lover.

One of the reasons for today's elevated divorce rate may be the unrealistic expectations with which many people approach relationships. In more traditional times and societies, people were less demanding of marital intimacy. Extended families, close communities, and religious institutions provided the needed support and sense of connection.

Lauren Bacall and Humphrey Bogart

LAUREN: No one has ever written a romance better than we lived it.

—*By Myself,* by Lauren Bacall

In contemporary Western society, individualism has reached new heights, making for unprecedented freedom but also eroding the social fabric that binds us together. Like Adam and Eve, our mythic ancestors, we are painfully conscious of our separateness from each other and from the material and spiritual worlds, and we long for atonement (at-one-ment) with that which transcends us. In passion, we think we have found the answer.

Although the tale of Tristan and Iseult suggests that a complete merger with another is not an earthly possibility, many still place their hopes for this—and more—on the fragile institution of marriage. In order to experience a true marriage, however, we must not lose ourselves or force our partner to do so by conforming to our expectations. Rather, through mutual respect and accommodation, both partners can achieve a transforming growth as individuals while maintaining a deep sense of connectedness to each other. Only then can we achieve real intimacy with the partner who will keep us company on our journey through life.

The Miracle *of* Love

Or How I *Failed* the Smelly T-Shirt Test

Steven Stosny

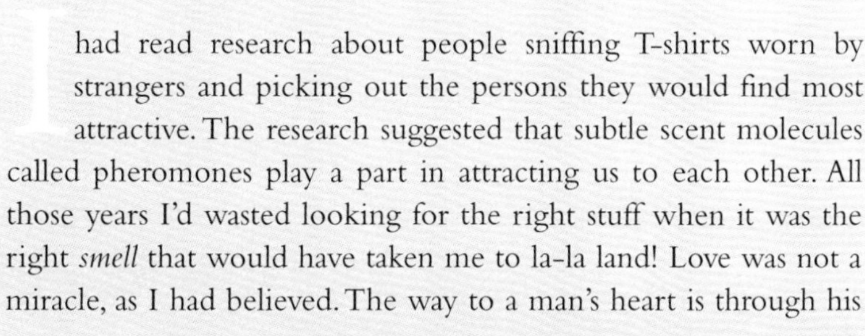

I had read research about people sniffing T-shirts worn by strangers and picking out the persons they would find most attractive. The research suggested that subtle scent molecules called pheromones play a part in attracting us to each other. All those years I'd wasted looking for the right stuff when it was the right *smell* that would have taken me to la-la land! Love was not a miracle, as I had believed. The way to a man's heart is through his nose.

It wasn't easy rummaging through soiled laundry baskets, sneaking into closets and drawers for clandestine sniffs, or pretending a woman had lint on her shoulder so I could cop a cheap smell as I removed it. I roamed subways, crowded streets, and amphitheaters in August, searching in vain for the sniff that would knock my socks off. I finally met someone in late autumn. But my little study was ruined. We both had colds.

Okay, perhaps love is a miracle after all—a spring-like rebirth from numbing routine, a kind of resurrection from the nearly dead, a blip on a dull screen that breaks the stillness of an emotional flat line. Even the initial phase, maybe stimulated by pheromones, certainly mediated by opium-like substances secreted in the brain (that give the walking-on-clouds high in her presence and physically painful withdrawal in her absence) is a kind of miracle. But it brings neither chronic euphoria nor surrender to a passion that knows no bounds. The miracle of love is unadulterated self-discovery.

The shame, fear, and core value in the depths of another's being stirs similar states in us. We discover ourselves by how we react to this window into another self, which serves as a mirror reflection of our own. Do we respond with love and compassion, withdrawal, or attack? No matter what attracts us, we grow to love those with the most benign mirror reflection—the ones who make us feel loving and lovable. The T-shirt study missed this point when it removed the possibility of rejection from its subjects. As rejection goes, so goes the nose.

The miracle of love is unadulterated self-discovery.

In the initial phase of love, self-discovery is euphoric; we realize how generous, giving, nurturing, open, flexible, passionate, intimate, competent, creative, and growth-oriented we have become. "You bring out the best in me," is as true as it is incomplete, for it is only half the miracle.

In time, the mirror reflection of love *must* show the whole picture of how petty, self-absorbed, ungenerous, rigid, shut down, cold, defensive, irritable, and manipulative we can be. I'm not talking about the *ashes* of resentment—things like drinking out of the milk carton or leaving the toilet seat up or forgetting to carry a glass into the kitchen. I mean the *fires* of resentment—how hard it is to sustain interest, to approach, listen, enjoy, learn from, and cherish, with anything like consistency.

And how irritable *she* can be! Most marital arguments are no more sophisticated than this: It takes one to know one. She doesn't care about me; she just cares about what I can do for her; she always has to be right; she never lets up; she doesn't understand me the way Cindy Crawford would.

She used to show me how wonderful I am, and now she shows me how wonder-less is my routine plodding through life. We all have one favorite mirror in the house—the one we go to in times of vulnerability that gently conceals most of the lines and blemishes. Did you even know what resentment *was* before you got married?

Love's relentless chipping away at its own narcissistic monument of the self as loving, lovable, masterly, tolerant, and successful is a crucial part of its self-discovery miracle, much like giving up the grandiose fantasies of adolescence. At five feet, six and one-half inches, I won the NBA championship on a last-second jump shot; I was Michael Jordan before Michael Jordan was Michael Jordan. And I thought that in love I could sustain interest, passion, trust, compassion, intimacy, and commitment indefinitely.

Love creates a narcissistic haze to trick us into thinking we're worthy of the miracle until the pain of reality *makes* us worthy. We become worthy by providing interest, compassion, trust, intimacy, passion, and commitment when it is needed, which, mercifully in most relationships, is not that often. We become worthy by recognizing that, on the most human level of core value, the best interests of self and loved ones are inseparable; we feel the most value when valuing the most.

To understand the miracle of love is to view it as if we are standing on a lone rock, looking up at the overwhelming infinity of a starry night. (The paradox of human nature is that we grow stronger by knowing our frailty and greater by accepting our insignificance.) In the grace of brilliant reality we experience the full miracle of love: appreciating the depth, breadth, wonder, and flaws of another human, in full acceptance of our own breadth, depth, wonder, and flaws. No nobler truth was ever wrought by smelly T-shirts.

Love creates a narcissistic haze to trick us into thinking we're worthy of the miracle until the pain of reality makes *us worthy.*

Love's Magic

When Embers Turn *to* Fire

George Doub

I was talking to my mother one time, telling her that I was looking for that special someone who would spark the fire of love in me. My mother's words were simply, "Remember, embers can turn to flame."

Most of us experience the flames—the chemistry of attraction and affection. But relationships are more than a blend of chemistry and affection; they are also a combination of skills and actions that are most often acquired in our families. So much of what we bring to our relationships originates in our families and culture with what we were taught and what we experienced—the routines, the language, the food, the styles for talking, and permission (or not) to touch.

Remember, embers can turn to flame.

Whether we come from more ritualized cultures, such as those of Asia and the Middle East, or from the more physical and verbal Latino and African American cultures, our families greatly influence three crucial processes in our ability to form and sustain loving and balanced relationships. These three processes—how we choose, how we speak, and how we touch—are sparked in our family.

CHOOSING MR. AND MRS. RIGHT

"We've always been a quiet family. We never fight. My parents just looked at me when I messed up."

"We grew up traveling all over to military bases. My family liked to move. I like to travel and meet new people; I like the exotic."

"I'm really most comfortable with my own kind . . . people from the same neighborhood or church, people who talk my language."

"I need someone who understands that we Cambodians take care of our parents in our home."

"I want my house to smell Mexican from the tortillas and food we eat."

Although images of our dream partners spring from many sources such as pictures, books, and movies, life within our family exerts a major influence on how we choose a life partner. Whether we do it consciously or not, when choosing a mate we look for connections to our roots. We build on the embers of our family fire. Perhaps banked or dormant, our heritage comes out under the pressure of choosing. Sometimes we choose the familiar—the food, color, language. Sometimes we build on our reactions to the way we were raised.

Quite commonly we choose someone just like our father or mother. We choose the familiar: someone who knows how to raise a family, someone who looks the same and speaks the same language. Many Latino and Asian men return to their country of origin in order to marry a *típica*—a woman who will cook their meals, have their children, and obey them. They choose a woman just like mom, who knows what to do and how to raise a family—and understands them.

Our families greatly influence three crucial processes in our ability to form and sustain balanced and loving relationships: how we choose, how we speak, and how we touch.

Even today in our country we have modern examples of people choosing their *típica.* Many people defer to their family's preferences, not just in terms of marrying within the same religion and ethnicity but, in extreme cases, by surrendering their choice altogether in arranged, "old country" marriages. Others choose someone they meet at work or church or within their circle of school and friends. In so doing, they start out with a shared history.

Still others look for the new, the exotic: Latinos choosing Anglos, Asians choosing Latinos, Anglos choosing African Americans. Three recently married couples I know of didn't even speak each other's language when they married!

SPEAKING THE LANGUAGE OF LOVE

"I love you. Let me hold you. I'm so proud of you."

"Here, take my hand and we'll walk together."

"It's OK; I'm here to take care of you."

"Of course you can snuggle. Good night."

"I really liked the way you took care of your sister."

"Tell it like it is."

"Thanks for coming to talk to me."

All homes teach the language of love—the mix of words, gestures, touches, glances, gazes, and winks that together convey feelings of closeness and affection. These prepare us to speak our own language of love.

Often our parents were unclear about what to say or how to say it, but if they demonstrated thoughtfulness and affection in their own relationships, we learned how to make it a part of ours. This was especially true when we were included in the circle of affection.

If our family was uncomfortable communicating affection and instead said things like "Be quiet," "Children should be seen and not heard," "Think before you speak," "Calm down," "Don't cry; be a man," then it becomes harder for us to develop facility in the language of love. Instead we may look for someone who either joins us in silent love or compliments our quietness.

When parents prepare us to be expressive, thoughtful, and affectionate (*cariñoso,* we say in Spanish), we have a better chance to develop a successful relationship. Children who hear their parents speak words of love, tenderness, and respect to each other and who also learn to do this themselves can develop the same language. The more we are encouraged to speak up, the easier it is to find the words and say them when we meet our special person. We can say, "*Te quiero, Te amo*" ("I love you"), "*Eres mi amor*" ("You are my love") and hear these words back.

THE RIGHT TOUCH

"Talk is cheap; actions speak louder than words."

"The moment we touched, I knew you were the one."

"What a great kisser. I love holding you and hugging you."

"Here, hold my hand."

"It's fun taking a bath together. Thanks for the foot massage."

When we touch, we bring together our different embers—the hormones, physical sensations, sexual attraction—and spark a new fire. An important element in building healthy relationships involves both touching and being comfortable with our bodies. Many families (traditionally, the Asian and Middle Eastern cultures) tend to avoid these taboo, sex-talk areas, whereas others (for example, the Latin and Polynesian cultures) are extremely comfortable with touching. For example, I remember a worker who bragged, "If I can just touch a woman, she'll be mine."

The mystery and the excitement of touching can ignite our fire. It can be a light touch, a gentle rub, a finger touching our cheek, tracing our ear, grazing our lips; just bumping together, holding hands, heads touching. And they are the right touches when we like it and when our partner likes it. Together these physical gestures become a kind of fuel that ignites and sustains our love fires.

Seeing our parents hug, kiss, hold each other, walk hand in hand, and look at each other teaches us to do the same. Seeing them comfortable with their bodies and able to talk to us about our bodies as we grow teaches us to be comfortable with our bodies and our sexuality. These experiences prepare us to touch in love and encourage the development of our own natural fire.

As we grow, we find balance in our relationships through the success and failures of friendships, dating, and perhaps finally of Mr. or Mrs. Right. Each time we listen closely to those we love and share ourselves openly and honestly with them in return, we move closer to building a loving relationship. What was our individual culture and family experience becomes our shared culture and experience. The embers become our flames.

What was our individual culture and family experience becomes our shared culture and experience. The embers become our flames.

The Search *for a* Soul Mate

Amy Gerson

When scanning the Personal ads in the newspaper, you may have encountered the phrase, "Searching for a soul mate." The term *soul mate* has recently become part of the pop culture vocabulary. A soul mate is one's emotional, intellectual, and spiritual twin. The concept of a soul mate is very appealing; it connotes wholeness and the end of one's longing and loneliness. In our culture's modern mythology, two soul mates fit together like two interlocking pieces of a jigsaw puzzle.

In fantasy I embrace the concept of the soul mate. But in reality I know that it is a purely romantic concept; if embraced literally, it will leave people with an enduring sense of emptiness and a lack of fulfillment. In truth, people's personalities have many facets, like a finely cut diamond. Finding one person who matches all your facets is simply not possible. Even in the best of relationships, partners inevitably become disappointed and can feel a sense of betrayal, anger, despair, and abandonment. As we gradually work through these feelings, we realize that one person alone can never fulfill us. Thus we require a variety of people in our lives. The best friend, professional colleague, tennis partner, confidante, co-shopper, and lover are just a few of the individuals who can be part of our lives. As a group these people may fulfill many of our needs. If we persistently chase the fantasy of the "other" who alone will fulfill us, we ultimately come face to face with our own emptiness.

Instead of searching for a life partner who is a soul mate, we need to search for a person we can connect with on those essential dimensions that we hold most dear. Family, work, religion, politics, mutual respect, caring, and "provision of safety" are examples of important areas. Sometimes a significant other may fulfill several of these needs, yet it is very rare to find a person who provides for all of them. I recently heard a humorous but very human anecdote from a woman who was scanning the Personals. She commented on an ad from a man whose main descriptor was that he liked sushi and walks on the beach. She reacted: "Can you build a life around sushi and walks on the beach?" Of course the answer is no! Sharing a lifetime with someone is infinitely more complex.

This leaves us with a choice: we can spend our lives trying to change the person we love—trying to make her or him fulfill all our needs—or we can accept the person's limitations and move to fulfill our diverse needs through a variety of other people. The internal side of the equation is that we must also deeply understand and accept who *we* really are! We need to confront our own wounds and fears, thus healing ourselves in the very way we expected help from our soul mate. It is easiest to love those qualities in another that are most similar to the ones we value in ourselves. It is much more difficult to love—even to truly accept—the differences. Ultimately what defines love is a profound acceptance of the differences. In accepting—and then learning to love—the differences, one transcends oneself (an experience of self beyond one's own limits and boundaries) and achieves a hard-to-define but very special spiritual peace. This realization does not lead to an ecstatic merger of partners but rather to a loving acceptance.

Ultimately what defines love is a profound acceptance of the differences.

We all search for a soul mate, hoping for emotional security and psychological restoration (the healing of our own wounds, doubts, and fears). We may have moments with a partner or a friend that can feel like a merger. These experiences are enjoyable but fleeting, and the notion that we can find enduring merger is a seductive psychological mirage that we never quite attain. All our love relationships turn out to be different from what we expect.

The solution to our soul mate hunger is paradoxical. If we can persist in a relationship with the realization that no one can be a fantasy soul mate, while learning to love the "otherness" of the other person, we ourselves will become more whole and truly capable of love. In some undefinable way, this important shift transforms us, our frustration and emptiness diminish, and we finally begin to feel fulfilled within ourselves. Thus we become able to be truly loving toward others.

Wisdom in Love

Henry Grunebaum

That love is all there is, Is all we know of love.

—Emily Dickinson

n all cultures for which there are adequate data,[1] romantic/erotic love is a well-documented experience.[2] It is a given. What differs among cultures is the place it has in how life is lived. Within any given culture, individuals deal with love very differently. We have all known people who are unable to experience romantic love and others who fall in love over and over. And cultures differ greatly in how they construct romantic love. In some, feelings of romantic love are the subject of fiction and movies but

Tell me where is fancy bred
in the heart or in the head.

—William Shakespeare,
The Merchant of Venice

are not acted on. For others, like the !Kung, an African Bush tribe, the feelings are experienced in affairs. And all over the world today, even in China,[3] romantic love is increasingly viewed as the preferred basis of committed adult relationships. I suggest that all these people must know something.

Why do people value romantic or erotic love as the basis of a committed adult relationship? Why not simply choose a sensible partner?

At this point, a story may be useful. In the late sixties, I counseled a number of couples from a poor section of Somerville, Massachusetts. The wife in several of these couples said, "He is a good husband," which I learned meant, "He does not hit me or the children, he doesn't drink, and he gives me his pay check each Friday night." One of these women told me, "I don't care much about sex, but it doesn't take anything from me and he seems to need it." I was bemused with the idea that for some people this was an adequate basis for a marriage.

Clearly a person encounters many sensible people to live with, and such a choice is certainly judicious. But for many people, sensible is not enough. And if it is not enough, what more is there? More sensible won't do, and something more is needed to bring two people together and keep them together through the vicissitudes of life—increasingly, a long life together. Pleasure, even sexual joy, is not enough; this experience can be had without any special emotional bond.

I do want to be clear that during their courtship most couples assess whether or not this relationship will be a sensible one, that is, whether the loved one is a wise choice. However, given the freedom to choose among many potentially sensible partners, romantic love becomes important in that choice. And it turns out that most people only meet a few others in a lifetime with whom they fall in love.[4] Romantic love is relatively rare.

It is also true that feelings of romantic love can get one in terrible trouble. One can end up with a totally unsuitable partner and gradually or suddenly find that the feelings wane and that nothing real is left to take their place.

> Oh, when I was in love with you,
>   Then I was clean and brave,
> And miles around the wonder grew,
>   How well did I behave.
> And the fancy passes by,
>   And nothing will remain,
> And miles around they'll say that I
>   Am quite myself again.[5]
>
> —A. E. Housman

It is also common that as a relationship continues, feelings of romance lessen and friendship, affection, and commitment become more important. Although romantic love lessens, one would hope it does not entirely disappear.

Because sensible is not enough and romantic love declines with time, we must ask, What special quality does romantic love have that makes it a wise choice? I suggest that this kind of love, uniquely, is transformative and fosters a particular kind of intimacy that leads people to feel known and feel that they know the other. It is also a much desired experience. "They say that falling in love is wonderful, it's wonderful, so they say," wrote Irving Berlin.

One of the fascinating aspects of the capacity for romantic love and its transformative effects is that these effects do not seem to wane with age. It is not clear whether children can feel romantic love. Certainly they can love peers and strongly so, but they usually do not have the language to describe it. A three-year-old boy in day care kisses my granddaughter, who seems to enjoy it. He is asked why he does this and replies, "I love M. She is so cute." However, with the onset of adolescence and sexual maturation, the capacity for romantic love comes into full bloom. And this potential continues throughout life. For example, a man in his seventies writes his therapist, who has helped him with the residue of two bad and abusive marriages, to relate that he has recently met his girl friend from college and they are "crazy in love again."

It is commonplace that the desire to be in love is so strong that people find it difficult to know whether what they are experiencing is a momentary fancy, a powerful sexual attraction, or "true love." And indeed, often time alone will make it clear what this passion is, and only gradually does the whole of the loved one become evident. As Francis Bacon said, "It is impossible to love and be wise."[6]

And yet another view:

> Love to faults is always blind.
> Always is to joy inclin'd
> Lawless, wing'd and unconfin'd,
> And breaks all chains from every mind.[7]
>
> —William Blake

When we are in love we feel better. We are wonderful because we are loved by the other, and we behave better both toward the other and, by extension, toward everyone else. We cherish the little tokens that belong to the other and remember events shared with the other. Commonplace things and events are endowed with special meanings. And it is a rare couple who, regardless of the current state of a troubled marriage, do not remember fondly the moment they met.

Probably the single most important effect of romantic love is that it expands one's universe to include another person, who becomes even more important than oneself.

Probably the single most important effect of romantic love is that it expands one's universe to include another person, who becomes even more important than oneself. It is this effect that leads people to seek love. "Love consists in this; that two solitudes protect and touch and greet each other."[8] And it is usual that this expansion of the human world is extended to include other people. "I was in love with the whole world and all that lived in its rainy arms."[9]

Almost everyone knows that although being loved is wonderful, even better is loving another. "The pleasure of love is in loving. We are happier in the passion we feel than in that we arouse."[10] It affords one the opportunity to transcend one's boundaries and to be selfless. "My bounty is as deep as the sea; My love as deep; the more I give to thee, The more I have," said Shakespeare's Juliet. Of course, parenthood involves a similar transformation, but here the other person is not an equal. Devotion and caring are not the same as dialogue and conversation.

In the context of love, sex becomes more than the gratification of bodily needs and pleasure; it is the physical continuation of conversation between lovers.

In the context of love, sex becomes more than the gratification of bodily needs and pleasure; it is the physical continuation of conversation between lovers.

It is striking that the Bible, when referring to sexual intercourse, states, "and he knew her." Now we would say that they "knew each other." The word *know* in the Bible means not only that the couple had sexual relations but that they knew and understood each other psychologically, and almost certainly that they cherished each other.[11] A long relationship is simply a long conversation—a way of knowing and cherishing the other—with all the differences, disagreements, comings together, and intimate sharing that interesting conversations have.

People all over the world are seeking romantic love because this kind of love allows one to know and be known by another. It may not always be sensible, but being known and knowing the other is more important than being sensible. Romantic love is both rare and precious—sensible alone may not be wise.

NOTES

1. Jankowiak, W. R., and Fisher, E. F. "A Cross-Cultural Perspective on Romantic Love." *Ethnology,* 1992, *31,* 149–155.
2. Recent research strongly suggests that romantic love is an attachment bond and is subject to the vicissitudes that attachment is affected by. For a fine review of this subject, see J. A. Feeney, *Adult Romantic Attachment and Couple Relationships,* pp. 355–377, as well as other chapters in Cassidy, Jude, and Shaver, *Handbook of Attachment: Theory, Research, and Clinical Application,* New York: Guilford Press, 1999.
3. Jankowiak, W. R. *Romantic Passion.* New York: Columbia University Press, 1995.
4. Grunebaum, H. "On Romantic/Erotic Love." *Journal of Marital and Family Therapy,* 1997, *23*(3), 295–307.
5. Housman, A. E. *The Collected Poems of A. E. Housman.* New York: Henry Holt, 1965, p. 31.
6. Bacon, F. *Essays of Love,* 1597–1625.
7. Blake, W. *Poems and Fragments from the Notebook,* 1793.
8. Rilke, R. M. *Letters to a Young Poet.* Translation by M. D. Herter Norton. New York: Norton, 1954.

9. Erdich, L. *Love Medicine.* New York: HarperCollins, 1984.
10. La Rochefoucauld, *Reflections,* 1678.
11. I have long wondered about the biblical use of the word *know* in the expression, "He knew her." Did it just mean sexual intercourse? So I discussed the issue with Professor Everett Fox of Clark University in Worcester, Massachusetts, who had recently done a groundbreaking translation of *The Five Books of Moses.* He confirmed that the use of the word *know* means both physical and psychological intimate knowledge; other words are used to describe rape and nonconsensual sex. In addition, the word is used in contexts that imply that when God knows his people, he cherishes them. Professor Fox thought this applied to couples as well.

Fools *for* Love

Steven Pinker

Why does romantic love leave us bewitched, bothered, and bewildered? Should we blame it on the moon, on the devil, on raging hormones? Or might there be a method to our madness?

People who study the nature of strategy have discovered a paradox: sometimes it pays to sacrifice your own self-interest and control. The eco-protester who handcuffs himself to a tree guarantees that his threat to impede the logger is credible; the prospective homebuyer who makes an unrecoverable deposit guarantees that her promise to buy the house is credible.

Social life is a series of threats, promises, and bargains, and economists such as Thomas Schelling and Robert Frank have suggested that some of these paradoxical tactics may have been wired into our nervous system by the forces of evolution. Offering to spend your life and raise children with someone is the most important promise you'll ever make, and a promise is most credible when the promiser can't back out. That idea provides insight into the strange logic of romantic passion, explaining it as a tactic to enhance a person's chances of attracting an optimal mate.

Unsentimental social scientists and veterans of the singles scene agree that dating is a marketplace. Everyone agrees that Mr. or Ms. Right should be good-looking, smart, kind, stable, funny, and rich. People shop for the most desirable person who will accept them, and that is why most marriages pair a bride and a groom of approximately equal desirability. The 10s marry the 10s, the 9s marry the 9s, and so on. Mate shopping, however, is only part of the psychology of romance; it explains the statistics of mate choice but not the final pick.

Somewhere in this world of five billion people there lives the best-looking, richest, smartest, funniest, kindest person who would settle for you. But your dreamboat is a needle in a haystack, and you may die single if you insist on waiting for him or her to show up. Staying single has costs, such as loneliness, childlessness, and playing the dating game, with all its awkward drinks and dinners (and sometimes breakfasts). At some point it pays to set up house with the best person you have found so far.

Your dreamboat is a needle in a haystack, and you may DIE SINGLE *if you insist on waiting for him or her to show up.*

But that calculation leaves your partner vulnerable. The law of averages says that someday you will meet a more desirable person, and if you are always going for the best you can get, on that day you will dump your partner. But your partner has invested money, time, and childrearing and has forgone opportunities in the relationship. If your partner was the most desirable person in the world, he or she would have nothing to worry about because you would never want to desert. But failing that, the partner would have been foolish to enter the relationship.

Look for a partner who is committed to staying with you because you are you.

Marriage laws offer some protection, but our ancestors had to find some way to commit themselves before the laws existed. How can you be sure that a prospective partner won't leave the minute it is rational to do so—say, when a newly single Tom Cruise or Cindy Crawford moves in next door? One answer is: don't accept a partner who wanted you for rational reasons to begin with; look for a partner who is committed to staying with you because you are you. Committed by what? Committed by an emotion—an emotion that the person did not decide to have and so cannot decide not to have—an emotion that was not triggered by your objective mate-value and so will not be alienated by someone with greater mate-value—an emotion that is guaranteed not to be a sham because it has physiological costs like tachycardia, insomnia, and anorexia—an emotion like romantic love.

It is often said that people who are sensible about love are incapable of it. Even when courted by the perfect suitor, people are

Tom Cruise and Nicole Kidman

TOM: It was lust at first sight. I felt a connection to her the moment I met her.

—*Ladies Home Journal,* November 1998

unable to will themselves to fall in love, often to the bewilderment of the matchmaker, the suitor, and the person him- or herself. Instead it is a glance, a laugh, a manner that steals the heart. Research on identical twins suggests that the spouse of one twin usually is not attracted to the other; we fall in love with the individual, not with the individual's qualities. The upside is that when Cupid does strike, the lovestruck one is all the more credible in the eyes of the object of desire. Murmuring that your lover's looks, earning power, and IQ meet your minimal standards would probably kill the romantic mood, even though the statement may be statistically true.

The way to a person's heart is to declare the opposite: that you're in love because you can't help it. Concerned parents and politicians notwithstanding, the sneering, body-pierced, guitar-smashing rock musician is typically not singing about drugs, sex, or Satan. He is singing about love. He is courting a woman by calling attention to the irrationality, uncontrollability, and physiological costs of his desire: "I want you so bad, it's driving me mad; Can't eat, can't sleep; I like the way you walk, I like the way you talk."

Of course one can well imagine a woman not being swept off her feet by these proclamations (or a man, if it is a woman doing the declaring). They set off a warning light in the other component of courtship: smart shopping. Groucho Marx said that he would not belong to any club that would have him as a member. Usually people do not want any suitor who wants them too badly too early, because it shows that the suitor is desperate (so they should wait for someone better) and because it shows that the suitor's ardor is too easily triggered (hence too easily triggerable by someone else). The contradiction of courtship—flaunt your desire while playing hard to get—comes from the two parts of romantic love: setting a minimal standard for candidates in the mate market and capriciously committing body and soul to one of them.

MEANING

Relationship *and* Other Difficulties

James Hollis

The older I get, the more problematic and fragile relationships seem to be. To have a relationship worthy of the name is precious, rare, and, for all the difficulties, a necessary developmental vision to which we must all be devoted. The paradox of relationship seems based on the dilemma that we can achieve no higher relationship to the Other than we have achieved with ourselves. A relationship, however, is required for the dialectic which, through engagement with the otherness of the Other, obliges us to grow beyond the limits of our reflexive, neurotic, defensive, repetitive, regressive, and history-bound personalities.

The chief fantasy that destroys relationship is the imposition of the search for a Magical Other who will heal us, protect us, and spare us our own individuation task. When the Other fails, as every mortal shall, to be the de facto "good parent" that such a fantasy posits, most relationships fall into the slough of despond and the problem of power. As Jung noted, where power prevails, love is not.

Although there are some persons with whom it is more appropriate to undertake a relational journey than others, there is no Magical Other. The quixotic quest for the Magical Other, which is the chief propellant of popular culture and romantic fable, achieves the desired fusion at the expense of the individual. Relinquishing the implicit quest for the parent is essential for a person to grow up, become a person, and, as Freud suggested, bear the normal miseries of life.

For a relationship to survive, one needs luck, grace, patience, and an enormous devotion to personal growth.

*For a relationship to survive, one needs **luck, grace, patience,** and an enormous devotion to personal growth.*

Luck suggests that the world is replete with absurdities, variables, and complexities that can empower or destroy persons and thereby relationships. We are in the hands of the gods, whether we will it or not, and much lies outside our control.

Grace asks a strength of character that enables us to forgive ourselves for our stupidities, cruelties, ignorance, narcissism, and wounding, and forgive our partners for the same. As theologian Paul Tillich defined *grace,* "Accept the fact that you are accepted despite the fact that you are unacceptable."[1] We are, and our partners are, only frightened travelers, fragile, easily hurt, easily intimidated by the loud roar of the universe and most needful of magnanimity of spirit. Touching, forgiving, accepting, and comforting oneself and the Other brings grace into this wounded world.

Patience is the necessary companion of *grace*. The work of relationship is never finished, vigilance never concluded, renewal never ended. Patience means sticking something out because it is so important. Sometimes relationships must be ended because they are too hurtful or they impede the individuation imperative, but relationships that still flicker with the spirit of hope, resilience, and purpose demand fidelity and constancy of purpose; they demand that we continue to show up and be accountable.

Personal growth is not deferred because one has a relationship; quite the contrary. The best thing we can do for our partners is to present them with a more evolved and interesting person with whom to be in relation.

The best thing we can do for our partners is to present them with a more evolved and interesting person with whom to be in relation.

The four principles that constitute the inevitable dynamics of relationship are

1. What we do not know about ourselves or will not face in ourselves will be projected onto the Other.
2. We tend to transfer our childhood wounding, our infantile longing, and our individuation agenda onto the Other.

3. Since the Other cannot and should not carry our wounds, our narcissism, and our summons to personhood for us, the relationship falls into the problem of power.

4. The best thing one can do for relationship, therefore, is to take full responsibility for one's infantile longing and for the individuation task.

This last assumption of responsibility is heroic in character—the chief requisite for truly loving another—and is the single most important dynamic in the healing and furthering of relationship. When one has let go of the search for the Magical Other, let go of the sabotaging hidden agendas, then one begins to encounter the immensity of one's own soul and of one's own journey. When the purpose of relationship is seen, then, not as finding a good caretaker but as a mutual commitment to support the growth of each Other, then we are in an enlarging, developmental, dynamic process that merits the name *relationship.*

NOTE

1. Tillich, P. *The Shaking of the Foundations.* New York: Scribner, 1948, p. 162.

Falling in Love with Love

Frank Pittman

ny damn fool thing anyone does, however suicidal or homicidal, is considered sacred—as sacred as cows are in India—if it is done in a state of in-loveness. Someone running from marriage, children, and adulthood might justify it by saying: "I was not in love with my husband, and if I had stayed when I was not in love I might have been miserable. You wouldn't want me to stay married for the children's sake?" Well actually, yes. But it is not sufficient just to stay married for the children's sake; it is necessary to stay happily married, lovingly married for the children's sake and for your own. And that doesn't require you to be in love but to be loving—to just do it.

Being in love has nothing whatever to do with loving someone. People who love make themselves feel good about themselves and enhance their sense of honor and integrity by making life better for others and by considering other people's feelings to be as important as their own. They are likely to be loved in return and live happily ever after, finding excitement in work and play instead of inflicting pain on their loved ones or blowing their lives apart.

Happiness . . . comes much more from the love we give than from the love we get.

In the 1996 film version of Scott McPherson's play "Marvin's Room," Diane Keaton, after a lifetime tending aged and infirm relatives, is dying. She talks to her sister, played by Meryl Streep, who has spent her life selfishly and frantically falling in and out of love with passing men.

KEATON (beaming radiantly): Oh, Lee. I've been so lucky. I've been so lucky to have Dad and Ruth, to have such love in my life. You know, I look back and I've had such love.

STREEP (uncomprehendingly): They love you very much.

KEATON: No, that's not what I mean. No, no. I mean that I love them. I've been so lucky to be able to love someone so much.

Happiness—the sort of happiness that gets us through to the end with pride in how we have lived our lives—comes much more from the love we give than from the love we get.

Joseph Barth

Marriage is our last best chance to grow up.

—*Ladies Home Journal,* April 1961

In-loveness has nothing to do with happiness. It is an obsessional state, partly fueled by anger and defiance, partly by a suicidal impulse. It's an adrenaline rush, like bungee jumping or shark wrestling, but more dangerous; the greater the pain and risk, the more intense the in-loveness. Falling in love with someone who is unavailable or when you are unavailable, working up a fantasy of escape from the reality of life and commitments, and then going to war with the real people in your life in order to disqualify them, escape them, and float off into la-la land to live out the fantasy, is a suicide equivalent for people who can't face living their real lives but aren't quite ready to die.

People intoxicated by in-loveness have not just disdain but actual fear of the comfortable, mundane happiness that awaits back in reality if the romantic spell is broken. In John Patrick Shanley's screenplay for the 1987 film "Moonstruck," Nicholas Cage seduces his brother's fiance, Cher, by explaining the relationship between love and happiness: "We're not here to be happy—we're here to ruin ourselves, to break our hearts, to love the wrong people, and to die."

The eighteenth-century German romantics, Goethe and Schiller, praised the suicidal nature of in-loveness in novels of astounding popularity. Goethe, in his first novel, had his overly sensitive young hero Werther kill himself for unrequited love, and it quickly became the trend for romantic young men to get themselves up in blue coats and yellow vests and demonstrate their sensitivity by likewise dying for love. Schiller, in his first play, "The Robbers" (the basis for Verdi's opera "I Masnadieri"), had his hero murder his beloved at their wedding altar to protect her from sharing his shameful life as an outlaw and to give her the sublime fulfillment of dying for love.

Nineteenth-century romantic heroines like Madame Bovary and Anna Karenina, finally liberated and free to choose their own mate, could throw their lives away on any man they fancied and thereby taste the ultimate freedom of choice. Romantics believe that the secret of happiness lies in freedom from reason and logic and responsibility and order. Therefore the choice that is most unreasonable, illogical, irresponsible, and disorderly must be the most liberating. If a choice seems wrong enough, then it must be right. Such is the nature of romance, in which sex, pain, sacrifice, and death are intertwined. There is no sane way to keep in-loveness alive—it must inevitably burn itself out and expose the reality of the pain and mess left in its wake.

The only way to keep in-loveness alive is to die at the point of orgasm, as spiders and operatic sopranos are wont to do. All the great love stories, from Tristan and Isolde and Romeo and Juliet to "Titanic" and "The English Patient," end with the death of one or both of the mismatched partners.

Adolescents, who have too much life in them anyway, love to give life up for love. Romance, like other adolescent illnesses, is far more dangerous for grown-ups, who may well confuse it with something real and important like marriage. In my forty years as a marriage therapist, I've treated about ten thousand marriages and several thousand divorces. Established first marriages rarely end in divorce unless someone has been unfaithful and tried to keep the affair secret or continue it. Affairs can occur in the best of marriages and in the worst, and most long-standing marriages are, at one time or another, both. People disoriented by the romance of an affair may confuse cause and effect and think the imperfect marriage caused the affair rather than that the affair wrecked the intimacy and made the marriage adversarial. Many people who have affairs come to their senses in time, but those who try to turn an affair into a marriage usually fail. Fantasy and reality are quite different realms.

It truly is magical to find your soul mate. . . . It is as magical as a manic episode or a demonic possession.

Bad therapists ask sufferers to compare the magical fantasy of an affair with the reality of a marriage. Writers of bad self-help books give hints on how to get the fantasy back into a marriage and, presumably, the reality out. Writers of bad advice columns respond to letters from readers who have fallen in love with their sister-in-law, the paper boy, or a convicted serial killer on death row, by urging the reader to examine his or her heart and determine whether this is true love. Presumably, denying true love would upset sufferers; it would cause a broken heart and a state of romantic tragedy. People pout when told they're nuts.

It truly is magical to find your soul mate, someone with whom your horoscope meshes, who shares your favorite song and your favorite color, who barely knows you and is just as crazy as you are and wants to run off with you and help you destroy your life and loved ones. It is as magical as a manic episode or a demonic possession. Fortunately it is a state of temporary insanity; it will pass.

But it is even more magical to have a partner whose past and future are inevitably intertwined with your own, who knows you, warts and all, and is willing to love you anyway.

Getting a Kick Out of You

The Jazz Taoist Key to Love

Peter Fraenkel

To answer the question, What do you believe the key to relationship success is? I draw on jazz and Taoism. Although these two cultural traditions originated at different points in history and on different sides of the globe, they share much common wisdom. Both jazz and Taoism revel in spontaneity, in seeing things afresh, in immersing oneself in the creative moment, and in paring down life to its simplest core. And both apply this approach to life in relationships.

Let's take jazz first. I think the Cole Porter song "I Get a Kick Out of You" sums up the key to happy relationships.[1] We need to see and deeply enjoy the uniqueness of our partners—to really let go of self-involvement for a moment or two and enter fully into experiencing the other, our partner. Lao Tze, the founder of Taoism, put it this way: "From wonder into wonder, existence opens." We need to be filled with a child-like open wonder as we see our partners being themselves.

I'm not talking about appreciating the big moments—our partner's major successes and achievements in the world or great surprise gifts to us. These are nice but not essential. I'm talking about the small gestures: how they roll over in the morning when they first wake up; how they look when they're caught off-guard, sneaking some ice cream from the fridge (or wrapping one of those great surprise presents); how they frown when they hear bad news—even how they cry when they're sad. These are moments when they're just being themselves, not focused on us. These moments are so important because they give us a chance to see who our partners are, apart from what they do for (or to) us.

It's really important that we get a kick out of how our partners handle both the emotional highs *and* the lows. The sign that you're getting a kick out of the lows might be finding yourself laughing gently and kindly when your partner is upset about something. He or she might look up quizzically, with a scrunched forehead, maybe even with an expression on the way to hurt, and say, "What are you laughing at?" And your honest answer is, "I'm not laughing at you, honey. It's just that you're so cute, even when you're upset." The impulse to hug him or her shortly follows.

From wonder into wonder, existence opens.

George and Barbara Bush

GEORGE: Love is never saying you have to be serious.

BARBARA: Did you make that up all by yourself?

—*LIFE,* February 1999

Professional, technical concepts such as *affect regulation, physiological soothing, conflict containment,* and *communication skills* are important, and I work with couples every day to develop these abilities. But it's all made much easier if each partner fundamentally *digs* the other—in the jazz, bebop sense. And that means digging the whole person—moods, reactions, and all. We're simply less reactive and frightened by our partner's moods when we see all of these as part of what gives us a kick.

Another important professional concept I value in my work with couples is the need for partners to achieve *intersubjectivity.* Simply put, this means they recognize and treat each other as truly *an other* consciousness and person rather than as *an object* to be manipulated into gratifying their own needs. This basically comes down to seeing the other with a sense of wonder—getting a kick from them as they are, free of distortions based on who we want (or fear) them to be.

The capacity to view one's partner with open wonder both requires and contributes to *acceptance*—another important concept in the contemporary couple therapy literature. In fact, getting a wonder-full kick from our partners often happens when we suddenly see and appreciate ways in which they are different from us.

When I speak of wonder, I don't mean awe. I reserve the experience of awe for feelings about God. And even though I believe that each of us is one of God's works, it's a bit hard to walk around in awe of your partner—hard on the neck muscles to look up all the time! Wonder (and its jazz affiliate, the kick) is an experience we can have looking (metaphorically speaking) straight ahead at our peer partner, on our level. Although it is important to respect our partners, respect without the wonder is like jazz without the swing, a lemon without the juice.

Respect without the wonder is like jazz without the swing, a lemon without the juice.

Let's face it. There are a heck of a lot of people we respect, but we wouldn't want to sniff their heads or jump in the sack with them!

While I'm on the topic of sniffing heads: there is no question that physical attraction is important in initially drawing us to our partners and in keeping that kick alive. But I'm far less impressed with the importance of the classic beauty criteria than I am with attraction on the intimate, sensual level—how our partners feel to touch, how they smell, how their mouths taste to kiss. Whatever researchers uncover about the role of pheromones and other biochemical messengers in attraction and love, on the experiential level I believe that digging the smell of our partners, and the taste of them, is a basic aspect of bonding.

Indeed one of the great shames of modern society is what I call the homogenization of beauty, that is, the belief that everyone must look like the latest fashion models to be considered beautiful, just so a bunch of companies can convince us we need their products. Aside from being terribly unfair to people whose body types couldn't possibly fit into the sterile forms of today's fashions, it means we may miss seeing the ways in which our partners are truly beautiful. Take a good, soft look at your partner and at yourself. Aren't you both beautiful already, in your own way?

Once you find that partner who gives you a kick, the big question is, How do you keep love alive? First it helps if your partner gets a kick out of you, too! I believe that people need to find someone who loves them equally as much. One partner doggedly pursuing the other or trying too hard to convince the other to love, even if it results in marriage, puts the relationship at risk of falling apart once the usual pressures of life set in. Although relationship process is important, the person we pick (and who we are to them) is important, too. I can't imagine investing the time to learn problem-solving skills with someone who doesn't give me a kick!

I don't believe there's only one person in the world for each of us. The number of possible partners with whom we can get a kick depends on our general openness to life, to variety in experience, to wonder. Those with a narrower range of what excites them may find it harder to locate that special someone. Those with an aptitude for seeing the beauty in a number of people may have more possible partners but a tougher time sustaining an exclusive commitment. If you find yourself getting "kicked" right and left by the wonderfulness of others and then dreaming about what life could be like with them, turn back toward your partner; try to rediscover small and wonderful things about him or her, and work on the issues and tensions that block your ability to enjoy that person.

A big part of what keeps love alive is that these two people who get kicks from each other also get shared kicks out of some of the same things in the world around them. Although research would suggest that the differences are not as important as how couples talk about them, I believe that there needs to be a baseline of common interests, things appreciated and enjoyed, and sensitivities, values, and concerns that tie partners together. Otherwise, it's hard to find reasons to spend time together and hard to imagine building a life together.

I believe that when we can get a kick from our partners and see them with a sense of wonder, every little thing they do is a link to our deeper appreciation of the universe.

NOTE

1. Although Cole Porter was not a jazz composer per se, it's the versions of his song by Ella Fitzgerald and Frank Sinatra that come to mind.

The Harder You Fall, *the Farther* You Fall

Shirley P. Glass

The story of their courtship was romantic. They had both remained single for many years because they had never met anyone with whom they could imagine spending the rest of their life. An hour into their first date, each was convinced of having finally found a soul mate. Now it was three years later, and they were sitting in my office hoping to rescue their distressed marriage from the brink of divorce. The passion they had experienced in their early relationship had evolved into intense, escalating fights with physical and verbal abuse.

Having encountered so many couples who became profoundly disenchanted with their relationship after a captivating courtship, I have become cynical about the reliability of "love at first sight."

"Being in love" typically refers to the first stage in a relationship in which one idealizes the other person and projects romantic fantasies upon them. Movies, novels, and song lyrics popularize such misconceptions by glorifying a passionate love that develops despite tremendous obstacles or inappropriate pairing. And most operas end with the death of the lovers; a fourth act in which they'd settle down into a comfortable family life would lack drama and passion.

The harder we fall, the farther we fall. When we place the object of our love on a pedestal, the eventual reality of their flaws and inadequacies creates an intense plunge from the heights. Those who start out adoring each other may feel that what is actually a normal stage of disillusionment is a catastrophe from which the relationship can never fully recover. The more wounded and needy we are, the more difficult it will be to find that perfect person who will compensate for the injuries and missing pieces from our childhood. Furthermore, excessive vulnerability creates defensive maneuvers such as attacking or withdrawing when our feelings are hurt. When both people are in pain at the same time, there is no adult present in the room to empathize with each other's hurt child. The greater our expectations that our partner will be the source of our personal fulfillment, the greater will be our disillusionment.

That's why I urge couples to *grow in love* rather than fall in love. Too often, infatuation, sexual desire, or romance is mistaken for a mature love that will endure the passage of time. Pleasurable sex can create a strong attachment that motivates couples to resolve problems, but when passion fades, some couples realize that they have very little in common.

In order to grow in love, I believe that it's more important to *be* the right person than to *find* the right person. *Being* the right person means that our capacity to love becomes greater than or at least equal to our need to be loved. The more complete and fulfilled we are as an individual, the more capacity we have for growing to love any one of a number of potential partners. We can remain assured that we are lovable despite being disappointed by incomplete validation.

It's more important to BE *the right person than to* FIND *the right person.*

It's not that we have lower standards than others but that our love is based more in reality. Lowering our expectations and accepting imperfections increases satisfaction and nurtures our relationship. The sun doesn't rise and fall on whether our partner got us a Valentine card, particularly during tax season (I am married to a CPA). Reality-based love might best be characterized by a statement my husband once made in the middle of an argument in which I was defending my virtues in the face of his criticisms. He said, "Shirley, if I didn't think you were a wonderful person, do you think I could put up with all of the things about you I can't stand?"

An internal alarm goes off for me when I hear an emotionally detached wife or husband say to their partner, "I do love you, but

I'm not *in love* with you anymore." This statement is often a symptom of partners who have become involved in an extramarital relationship. Unfortunately, people who have affairs are confusing the excitement of a forbidden love with the routine and security of a long-term relationship. The stranger across the crowded room may make your heart beat faster, but chemistry is not a reliable predictor that you will end up as best friends. People having affairs often rewrite the history of their marriage in order to justify their betrayal. They say, "I realize now that you weren't the *right* person for me." They are often confusing the positive mirroring and idealization of a new romance with the tarnished images of a long-term relationship. The idealization of romantic love is like a vanity mirror with tiny bulbs all around the perimeter, reflecting a rosy glow. Reality-based love is more like the make-up mirror that magnifies our wrinkles.

Love grows when we can share our excitement in our interests and activities. However, we also need to develop separate interests and a separate self in order to bring outside energy into the relationship. Boating, hiking, and horseback riding are some people's favorite activities, but they all sound like Outward Bound for convicted criminals to me. I am a psychologist, and my husband is an accountant. We have been married for so many years that he suggests that his clients get into psychotherapy, and I counsel my patients to be sure to explore the tax consequences of their financial decisions.

Romantic love is like a vanity mirror . . . reflecting a rosy glow; reality-based love is more like the make-up mirror that magnifies our wrinkles.

I recently spent some time with my cousins, Beverly and Jack, who have been married forty-five years. Jack said that he knew he wanted to marry Beverly the first time he met her and that she was the best thing that had ever happened to him. He was attracted to her because they shared intellectual and artistic interests, and he admired her independent spirit. Their marriage has thrived because of their loyalty and mutual support. Their attraction was based on their accurate perceptions of each other's character, personality, and intellect. I am forced to admit that "love at first sight" does work for some couples, but "love is blind" does not work at all.

The Full Monty

Peggy Vaughan and James Vaughan

Love has many stages, each wonderful and unique. The Full Monty, however, is loving on *all* levels—body, mind, and spirit. Why settle for less than the full love experience?

Maybe you think that "falling in love" is as good as it gets. What a wonderful feeling! It's intoxicating and all-consuming. You can't think of anything else—and you can't keep your hands off each other. We still refer to the beginning of our own relationship at age sixteen as our period of "young, hot love," but of course these feelings aren't restricted to young people; they're typical of *any* new love at any age.

You may wish these feelings would never end, and you may go to great lengths to sustain them or to rekindle them when you feel them changing, but they simply don't last—at least not in that form. Even though falling in love is a fantastic experience, much of the intensity of the feeling is inherent in its newness and novelty.

The Full Monty is much more than just the initial physical connection. It includes the more mature mental connection that comes from being friends and sharing life's responsibilities—as well as the spiritual connection that comes from developing deep trust and intimacy through full disclosure to each other.

This spiritual connection is possible only through responsible honesty—really *knowing* each other by sharing your deepest hopes, fears, and dreams on an ongoing basis. This kind of honesty is much more than just "not lying"; it's "not withholding relevant information" from your partner, dropping all the barriers, and allowing deep intimacy. (And this kind of honesty can be sexier than all the sex manuals you can buy.)

Frankly, this level of deep trust and true intimacy cannot be reached quickly. It's quite different from the kind of intimacy that develops when people disclose themselves to each other on first meeting, with no shared history and no joint responsibilities at stake. That initial feeling of intimacy is what people often mistakenly refer to as "finding a soul mate."

There's no such thing as finding your soul mate. You become soul mates over time.

We thought we were soul mates when we connected as teenagers. We felt sure we had a special love that would hold us together, no matter what. But there's no such thing as *finding* your soul mate. You *become* soul mates only after establishing a full love based on connecting on all three levels—physical, mental, and spiritual. Unfortunately, it's quite rare for a couple to truly become soul mates. That's because it takes time, commitment, and experience.

Mel and Robyn Gibson

MEL: People are chasing things they can't get. They're just illusions. Too many people go into marriage too lightly. You've got to take it seriously. Go in there wanting to make it last. . . . It wasn't a huge romance straightaway. We became great friends first.

—*People Weekly,* 1996

And even if you do become soul mates, it doesn't mean your love is now fixed in place, never again to change. A vital love relationship is always changing and, ideally, growing. Although different aspects may be more dominant at one time than another, all are needed in some measure if a couple is to have the best of what love has to offer.

For instance, the strength of our initial physical love was enough to sustain us for quite a while. Then when we married, we added a serious, "grown-up" commitment to each other to make a life together. Although we had great love and formed a great partnership, it wasn't until we'd been married for eighteen years (and "in love" for at least twenty-one years) that we knew the spiritual aspect of love even existed. It was through facing a real crisis in our marriage (James's extramarital affairs, about which we have written extensively) that led us to this level. At that point we committed to a kind of rock-bottom honesty that laid the foundation for an unshakable trust and a truly spiritual connection.

Once we really got that, we've never wavered in our all-out commitment to honesty, to really knowing each other, to being connected in the world together. This kind of connection goes beyond being lovers; it goes beyond being married or being parents and grandparents or being friends or partners. It's a much more powerful connection that cannot be broken, no matter what.

Being connected on this much deeper level gives meaning to life and provides a firm place to stand in the world, allowing you to go out and face the world on a completely different basis than would otherwise be possible. By integrating your love for other special things in life with the love you feel for your partner, you can develop a loving way of being in the world.

However, even when you finally reach this point, it does not remain a fixed situation. There's a natural fluctuation in all three levels of a love connection—body, mind, and spirit. Sometimes the passion is high; sometimes it's low—often affected by the degree of stress related to differences in dealing with joint life responsibilities. Sometimes the partnership (in a practical sense) works well; sometimes you're at odds—often affected by the degree of physical closeness you feel at the time. But once you make the deep spiritual connection, that's not likely to waver.

So love is far more complex than our simple notions of romance or friendship or partnership. In fact, essential to experiencing the full force of love in our lives is learning to respect love's significance and clearly understanding just what's at stake. Love is not some little fringe issue that exists in isolation; it's part of your total world; it's a central force that is integral to your life as a whole.

When all is said and done, having a long-term, loving relationship ranks near the top of the list of the best of what life has to offer. So why settle for less? Why not go for the Full Monty?

On Love *and* Devotion

Charlie Verge

One of the greatest losses in modern and postmodern society is the loss of devotion. I have more frequently heard the word *devotion* used in my therapy office with reference to someone's work or to a cause than to one's partner. Although our culture still values being devoted to one's children, the very utterance of the word with respect to one's primary relationship conjures up notions of codependency, dependency, and "loving too much." This loss most likely has myriad sources, but two of the most obvious are a lack of devotional practice with respect to spirituality and the increasing emphasis on equality between partners. For at the heart of devotion is spiritual submission or placing oneself at the service of another.

This is a hierarchical relationship wherein one indeed places another above oneself, and loves and adores from that place.

At the heart of devotion is spiritual submission or placing oneself at the service of another.

Unfortunately, the history of relational abuse in our culture, particularly of women by men, has led to a widespread fear of hierarchy in relationships. Thus the best aspects of healthy spiritual submission in the devotional sense have been sacrificed for notions of mutual respect, autonomy, and "my lover as friend." When this same fear is transferred to God, devotion is replaced by social justice, ethics, and even spiritual disciplines such as meditation practice. I in no way want to diminish the value of these qualities in both spirituality and relationships, but although they are essential, they are only half of the equation. For true spiritual love is devotional and unconditional. It is willing to sacrifice. It is willing to put the other on a pedestal. It is willing to serve. Yes, it is even willing to submit.

On Magic and Mystery

One of the most enjoyable aspects of my participation with the couples who come to my office is hearing the stories of how they met and what attracted them to each other. These are beautiful stories, and I really like taking the time to elaborate them. If the couple isn't in too much pain or hopelessness, they enjoy telling them. Even if only for a short time, many couples can identify a time of magic—a time when they were experiencing attraction or falling in love, when something about the other or about the connection seemed to pull them together.

Some folks can articulate what it was that drew them; others express almost dumbfoundedness. Regardless, there seemed to be some chemistry or magic in the air. Sometimes that chemistry seems to have had its origins in childhood experiences. With others it's better characterized by certain personality traits that seem to balance, offset, or curiously fit one another. Whatever the source of the chemistry, it is simply uncanny as to the perfection of the fit. Having had the privilege of being allowed into the intimacy of this magic with hundreds of couples over the years, I continue to marvel at the design. In fact, many couple-therapists talk to each other about this perfection, wherein each person represents both the perfect "draw" for the other and the perfect "rub" in terms of vulnerabilities or unresolved issues.

Personal Love, Unconditional Love, and "The Crunch"

This initial attraction is very personal. It can include such small details as a person's dress, tone of voice, smell, height, hobbies, and jokes. We fall in love with a unique person—unique right down to their moles. This, however, is not unconditional love. On the contrary, it is very much conditional and based on the unique

Cokie and Steve Roberts

COKIE: I think the word is "devotion." There's a special level of affection that is based on longevity, on knowing each other well over a period of time and going through many things together, happy and sad.

—*USA Weekend*, January 2000

characteristics of the other. And right here is the beauty and genius of the design. The initial magic of love can pull us into devotion, which is the doorway into the essence of who we are as beings of unconditional love.

Here's how it seems to work. Those little things we love about the other stir up our devotion to the person who possesses them. Those very unique conditions in the other can pull us into our unconditional love through the doorway of devotion. It is the act of devotion that can then take us beyond both ourselves and the other into the heightened state of consciousness of unconditional loving. When two people are engaged in this joy together, it is difficult to know who is giving and who is receiving, as only the consciousness of selfless love is present.

But of course at some point in the evolution of the relationship there is a contraction, or a tendency to move away from this state of unconditional love. In addition to being souls intending to express our unconditional love, we are also personalities that have wounds and experiences of hurt, fear, mistrust, and the like. The uniquely personal qualities that first brought out our devotion are the very same qualities that will inevitably bring forth the contraction or pull away from the other. I have expressed this to students by saying that the point of first attraction will also be the point of first contraction or conflict.

And herein lies "the crunch." When the personal qualities that initially served as a basis for my personal love and devotion are removed, I am challenged in my level of unconditional loving. It is suddenly hard to be unconditional because the personal part, which was the foundation of my access to unconditional love, is taken away. But this very moment is where it is possible to grow spiritually in leaps and bounds.

Spiritual Love and Partnering

When personal love gets tested, it is difficult not to let our personal concerns take over and allow our love to take a back seat. Hurt, fear, anger, and a host of other feelings can lead us into reactive positions and negative expressions. Those personal conditions that once drew us into unconditional loving are now drawing us into very conditional love. And the contraction feels terrible. There is indeed anguish over the loss of one's own expression of love, which essentially is a loss of one's true self. But even though we may not like it, the fact remains that we grow spiritually when it becomes hard to stay loving unconditionally, not when it is easy.

We grow spiritually when it is hard to stay loving unconditionally, not when it is easy.

Here lies the spiritual growth opportunity of accessing one's loving nature at this most difficult and critical juncture. To expand in the face of this pull into contraction is the very act of spiritual healing. A lifetime of hurt and the patterns of behavior that emanate from that hurt can be transformed. Of course, this is much easier said than done, for there are always a host of very good reasons not to do it, and they are usually sitting there right across the dinner table. How, then, do we even begin to go about it?

Intention

The single most powerful tool I know is intention. I think of intention as the opposite of addiction. In addiction I surrender, usually unconsciously, to a negative pattern. With intention, I surrender to a heartfelt and consciously chosen, positive pattern that replaces the addiction. Regarding relationships, you have to have the intention in your daily life to be more loving, to be less controlled by your hurts, and to be more of who you truly are. Intention doesn't care about who the other person is or what he or she might have done. It cares only about growing in the capacity to be free to love in any situation, at any time. But what exactly would living this way look like if we could do it?

There is a great deal of confusion about what the nature of unconditional love is in a partnership. It is not about tolerating all behaviors in the other or accepting inappropriate actions or abuse. Unconditional love moves toward upliftment, not toward anything destructive. First and foremost it is unconditional in its love for oneself, and it seeks that in others as well. To set the intention of growing in one's love doesn't mean that you have to know how to do it or what shape it will take. In fact, it's better if you don't. For the intention itself can create freely whatever expression is necessary, be it talking more or less or louder or softer—or pursuing or dropping whatever it is. The key is that we have to be willing to submit to its action, letting love guide us or, to put it in spiritual terms, letting go and letting God guide us. And this is an act of devotion—devotion to ourselves and our true nature, devotion to our partner and their nature, devotion to love and its nature. For when that nature expresses itself, it has a glow about it that attracts our partner to it as well. And there we are falling in love again. It takes lots of practice and lots of generosity with ourselves falling in and out of it (another act of submission and devotion). But then again, what else do we have to do with our lives?

So let's not be afraid to set this intention for ourselves. Let's be willing to surrender to this intention. Let's allow ourselves to be devoted to our partners and allow that devotion to heal our lives and lead us home.

Afterglow

Scott M. Stanley

We live in a culture saturated with constructions of love defined as passion. Passion is dominant because passion is powerful. What person does not either desire it, bask in the glory of it realized, or grieve over the loss of it in life? Passion's potency arises from the promise, whether obtained or not, of the deep acceptance of one's soul. Passion hints at the possibility of a soul mate. But there is something more powerful than passion—something that passion is incomplete without.

For most people, passion at its height resembles something like the birth of a fire on dry wood: great fury and heat, crackling flames leaping high. The start of such a fire is magnificent. My focus here is not on the great fire but on the coals that are begun from it. It is the long-burning coals and embers that sustain the promise of heat and fire to come.

"It's as easy as falling in love." Perhaps you've used this expression to tell a friend how easy it was to learn or do something new. Falling in love is the easy part of it all. It's the flaming, blazing, rush of love. Passion. But it's seldom the sustaining part. Starting well is easy. Ending well takes something more.

I am not arguing against passion. A pitiful life it would be without the possibility or realization of it. However, what sustains the pile of coals with their promise and warmth? What is the force of the more complete love?

Falling in love is the easy part. . . . Ending well takes something more.

There are many answers one could give, but I want to focus on *sacrifice.* The word *sacrifice* has fallen into disfavor with the ascendancy of a focus on "me" in our culture. However, I think the concept will make a comeback for the simple reason that long-term love is not remotely possible without sacrifice—passionate or not. The glow in the coals is sustained by the gentle breeze of sacrifice.

In his book *The Brothers Karamazov,* Fyodor Dostoevsky used the character of Father Zosima to express great thoughts. Here is one of my favorite lines from that work:

> Love in action is a harsh and dreadful thing compared with love in dreams. Love in dreams is greedy for immediate action, rapidly performed and in the sight of all. Men will even give their lives if only

the ordeal does not last long but is soon over, with all looking on and applauding as though on stage. But active love is labour and fortitude, and for some people too, perhaps, a complete science.[1]

Goldie Hawn and Kurt Russell

GOLDIE: We're individuals who, every day of our lives, wake up and choose to be together. That's a very different dynamic. It's empowering.

—*Good Housekeeping,* April 1999

Active love, he says, is a "labour" and a "fortitude." It's gritty, enduring, resilient love. Love in dreams is wonderful. When dreamy love enters the confines of time and space, it can arouse places in the soul like nothing else. Sparks fly. However, Dostoevsky implies that it is fleeting and can be vain. It is also the easy part. You do not "switch on" passionate love; it switches you on. Sometimes it switches on you. Wild fire.

Such love does not have to be fleeting. For too many couples, it is made to flee in the face of cruel slings and arrows. Whether or not most couples can sustain passionate love has often been debated. But I am sure that no couple sustains it for long without wedding it to the harder-edged love that is based on sacrifice. To push the metaphor, the only couples who can ignore tending the coals are those who have an endless supply of wood to throw into the flames. Coals don't matter if you always have flames.

To use Dostoevsky's term, *active love* is that which will require you, at some point, to put aside self-interest in favor of the good of the other and the relationship. I have been puzzled for years about Dostoevsky's point that active love (which I believe is enacted in various types of sacrifice) is to some "a complete science." Dostoevsky wrote in a time when science held an almost mythical promise to improve life for human beings. However this promise has been realized, what good science does is yield more complete understandings that can lead to better devices and better decisions. Perhaps Dostoevsky's point here was that active love is more complete than love in dreams. I believe the fundamental ingredient of this more complete, active love is sacrifice in its various expressions.

In an important way, sacrifice balances passion in the hearth of love.

What does passion lack that sacrifice makes up for? Passion lacks the ability to be directed by your will. That's probably why we are all so deeply affected by passion—it is captivating. Sacrifice comes from the active, choosing part of love based in your will. You can choose to love in this way because you can choose to do loving acts. In an important way, sacrifice balances passion in the hearth of love.

I realize that the word *sacrifice* conjures up images for many that are unpleasant. Perhaps an animal sacrifice comes to your mind, or a marriage in which one relatively victimized partner chronically gives up all for another who is nothing more than a selfish lout—or worse, a brutish tyrant. I am not addressing such matters here. The aspect of love I wish to call to mind is far grander and more noble, yet most often acted upon in the smaller stages of life.

The range of behaviors that can reflect a loving sacrifice is great. A few examples:

- When one chooses to forgive another for some past hurtful deed
- When one responds gently and with care to a vulnerable aspect in the other, even when this aspect is not attractive to gaze upon
- When one chooses to go to the movie the other most wants to see when it is not the one more personally desired
- When one decides with force of will *not* to return a negative comment, even when believing the partner lashed out to harm
- When one decides that some gain in the realization of the other's dreams in life is worth some loss in one's own

I have seen many unwise acts of sacrifice that epitomize "casting pearls before swine." There are many appropriate expressions of these concerns. But I am far more troubled about a culture that obscures an important truth with its focus on "me." The truth is that, for most couples, a variety of sacrificial gifts are needed to sustain any hope of real, lasting love. Surely there is no opportunity for passion to stay kindled when there is no harder, deeper love being worked out in the coals. This is love that acts to bless the other.

NOTE

1. Dostoevsky, F. *The Brothers Karamazov.* New York: Barnes & Noble, 1995, p. 50.

Embracing *the* Nature *of* Love's Sacred Journey

Dee Watts-Jones

'm feeling you" is an expression among many African American youth—one that I have come to love. It is an expression with multiple shades of meaning. When a young black manchild said this to me in response to a point I had made, I felt that we had *connected*. I knew that he had understood me cognitively, but to "feel me" was to connect with me intimately on an emotional level as well. What a wonderful way to convey understanding—a way that privileges understanding at a feeling level. It is a way that allows for being "touched" or "moved" in our understanding.

On another occasion I was approached by a young black man who said, "I'm feeling your locks," referring to my hairstyle. What

I understood is that he was resonating, connecting with the beauty of my hair. He was "feeling it." What a wonderful way to extend the experience of beauty beyond the visual to one of the emotional. These expressions remind me once again of the ingenious and creative use of language in the African American community. The words remind me of the strong value we place on feeling and relating to others at this level. They also remind me of *love.*

I do not pretend to know what love *is,* any more than I know what God is. Love and God are to me "The Great Mystery"—an expression coined by Native Americans. Still I know love and God. I have experienced their presence, and I know some things about them. I know, for example, that they are inseparable and that this is true whether or not someone believes in God. I know love to be an intense, passionate form of "feeling someone," of connecting emotionally and spiritually with another. To be conscious of the *spiritual* connection is to experience the richness of that connection as part of a shared spiritual journey—a journey of connecting with their divine purpose and to all there is.

I know love to be a process of *opening.* It is a process I believe to be boundless. It is *opening* to all parts of oneself—the glorious and the craziness—and to the loving kindness of God that reminds us that we are worthy, just as we are. It is

> *Opening* to our softness, our vulnerability, pain, and uncertainty, our ability to forgive, our kindness, our human-ness
>
> *Opening* to these same places in others, especially in our partner

Opening to unconditional friendship

Opening to the beauty of life, to a smile, a bluejay, the sound of rain, the sensual

Opening to the new, the different, the expansions and contractions, the impermanence, the variation of life

It is *opening* that allows us to be conscious, to connect, to give and receive, and to grow. It is both wonderful and frightening. We fear what we may find or feel and what others may see, or feel, about us. We fear our nakedness. It is therefore an act of courage and trust when we open. The trust is in our ultimate safety. Are we safe with ourselves and with God?

Opening is the water of relationship, the "feeling you," the nurturance, renewal, fluidity, and depth.

I know love to be erotic. Here I am using erotic in the way Audre Lorde does in her essay, "Uses of the Erotic: The Erotic as Power" as "a kind of energy that heightens and sensitizes all my experience."[1] In a partner love relationship, the erotic includes a sexual energy—a desire to express passion and connection through physical pleasuring. The deeper the level of opening within the couple, the more

in
you grew
into my life
sub
subliminally
seeping in
titrated infinitely
with patience
&
certainty.
a vapor
without witness
odorless. . .
travelling
thru the land
of my temple
curling around
the neurons
&
woven
in the marrow
long
before i knew
u solid
parting rivers
down
my spine.

—thandiwe

spiritual communion there is in their physical communion. This physical resonating is the fire of relationship—attracting, energizing, releasing, and "smoking" (pronounced ssmmohk-ing). In African American jargon, a person "smoking" is doing something intensely, passionately, and oh so well.

I know love to be light-hearted. Even in its intensity, love has the capacity to relax, to lighten up, and see the humor in things. Love rejoices in itself. It is playful, silly, and full of laughter. Love is fun. This is the air of relationship—light, easygoing, and sustaining in an imaginative, sometimes mischievous way.

I also know love, if it is to flourish, to be a process of commitment—commitment to the work of relationship, a conscious investment in continually *practicing* the work of relationship. Loving someone is an experience that happens and one that we learn how to do. To sustain love, we have to learn how to negotiate everything—time, space, and differences of all kinds, and to do this respectfully. We have to learn how to see more "and" than "or." We have to keep practicing *opening*. We have to learn how to speak to each other in ways that allow us to be heard, that allow us to be received. We have to practice being *present* to the other, even in the moments of alienation. We have to practice balancing, especially the "I" and the various "we's." Commitment to the work of love is the earth of relationship—the solidity, the plowing.

Love relationships are powerful teachers, and I believe that those love partnerships that go on living for years are those in which there is much for each to teach and learn from the other.

There is no doubt in my mind that this is an intersection of divine order and partners' readiness for love's many dimensions. Most inspiring to me are those love partners who are conscious of their spiritual partnership. They are committed to their own and each other's spiritual growth and to honoring and sharing their divine gifts with the community of life. They are committed to deepening the *opening,* trusting more and fearing less.

> when flesh and flesh
> meet
> nothing can stop
> their union
> when heart and heart
> meet
> nothing can stop the
> passion
> when soul and soul
> kiss
> who can stop the
> love?
>
> —Afua Cooper[2]

NOTES

1. Decosta-Willis, M., Bell, R. P., and Martin, R. (eds.). *Black Erotica.* New York: Doubleday, 1992, p. 81.
2. *Black Erotica,* p. 241.

MARRIAGE

Marriage *as a* Beautiful Ordeal

Stephen Gilligan

ow many marriages or committed relationships do you think you have in you? Before you answer, let me tell you a story that my friend Bill O'Hanlon, the noted author and psychotherapist, told me.

Bill was engaged to be married and was looking for hints about how to have a successful marriage. In his inimitable fashion, he tried talking with just about anyone who had succeeded in a long-term relationship. One night at a party, some friends pointed out an older couple, saying they had been happily married for fifty years. Bill approached the woman at one point, introduced himself, mentioned his situation, and wondered whether the woman could share any of her secrets for a happy marriage. The woman looked

Al and Tipper Gore

TIPPER: Good marriages don't just happen—they take a lot of love and a lot of work. When things get rough, you don't just cut and run.

—*LIFE*, February 1999

at Bill and exclaimed, "Young man, I don't know who told you that I was married to the same man for fifty years. I've actually had five husbands over the past fifty years!"

An embarrassed O'Hanlon listened as the woman described her first husband. He was a romantic, thoughtful man who took her out to romantic dinners, wrote love letters, and went for long walks with her. When they had their first child, she said, that man left her. She was very angry and had to adapt to her second husband, a hard-working man who was a responsible provider, worried about money, and didn't write love notes. In time she grew to love this man and was thus very upset when *he* left her and she acquired a third husband. Somewhere between the descriptions of her third and fourth husbands, it finally dawned on Bill that this woman was talking about the same man! With the same man she had experienced five distinct marriages, five distinct husbands. Each marriage had a beginning, a middle, and an end. Each was connected by a death and rebirth process.

This story has been helpful in my own marriage of fifteen years, as it has been for many other couples I have worked with. We all know the first stage of a relationship: romance, hope, "true love," bliss, a feeling of communion and ease. We also know the second stage, when the "romance drug" wears off. We're upset that our partners didn't fully heal us or save us or come through on the many promises that (we thought) they had made, both explicitly or implicitly. Kids and jobs distract us, arguments don't get resolved, resentment and frustrations set in, acting out (through sex, drugs, or rock 'n' roll) may happen. Maybe death, loss, and tragedy hit hard. We are left with many feelings: anger, depression, boredom, helplessness, numbness.

This is when the inevitable happens: a relationship dies. It is often a painful, difficult death—not a physical death but a psychological or spiritual one. A death of hope. A death of childhood longings for one's partner to heal wounds. A death of the isolated ego. A death of the first part of your life. A death that, when permitted to happen and given proper attention, allows for the rebirth of a marriage into a third stage: a conscious relationship based on deep listening, mutual support, mature intimacy, and lots of fun.

All this brings up questions: Are you willing to die? Are you willing to be born again in a new relationship quite different from your original understandings? I hope the answer to both questions is yes because I think that's what is necessary for a mature, loving relationship.

We are conditioned, of course, to avoid and fear both death and loss at all costs. Consumerism requires an eternal adolescence of energetic smiling, a vow to avoid pain at all costs, and a conspiracy to deny the shadow side of life. As a result, when a couple sails into the deep (and dangerous) waters of "our (current) relationship is over," they assume they are irretrievably off course. Finding themselves unhappy, they believe that the only chance for happiness is with someone or something else. Sometimes this makes sense. If a person really isn't right for you or is treating you badly, it may be best to leave. But whether you leave or stay, the same issues may await you in the next relationship. So if it's at all possible, stay and find a way to be reborn.

This doesn't mean resigning yourself to a bad situation; on the contrary, it means committing yourself to finding new ways to respect both yourself and your partner in the marriage. Amazingly, the worst feelings you have may help you the most in this process. They are telling you that something's not right, that something inside of you needs to be listened to and respected, that your old ways of thinking and acting aren't working. For example, a depressing feeling may tell you that "it's no use; nothing works." By listening to that feeling with curiosity rather than pessimism, you may find that behind it is a deep desire to feel closeness with your partner. ("I want to feel nurturance, but I haven't yet experienced it.") Rather than assuming that it will never happen or that it isn't happening because of something wrong or bad with you or your partner, accept that whatever you've tried so far hasn't worked. The depression may be telling you that your learned understandings of how to give or receive nurturance—for example, by always trying to be nice or by critically demanding it of your partner—are unworkable. By accepting that, you begin to open yourself to new possibilities about how to foster nurturance in yourself and in your marriage.

By opening yourself to learning from your negative emotions, you can begin to make the ordeal of marriage a positive and rewarding one. Nothing quite prepares you for the long road of death, rebirth, and transformation. In fact, much in consumerism and pop psychology misleads you about it. So while you're hoping that things will get happier, happier, happier, it's quite a shock when things crash. You think you've failed; you think there's no hope; you think it's over.

But "death," in the psychological and spiritual sense, is supposed to happen. Difficulties are supposed to happen. Struggles are supposed to happen. Doubts, disillusionment, and crises are inevitable.

What's the point of the ordeal? To get you to grow up, nothing less.

What's the point of the ordeal? To get you to grow up, nothing less. To get you to surrender your ego and give birth to a Self. (As Jung used to say, "The experience of the Self is always a defeat for the ego."[1]) To access childhood wounds and experience a healing relationship. To transfer your deepest commitments from your first family to your chosen one. To learn how to listen, to nonviolently negotiate, to find a middle way between domination and submission. To become a human being in a human community.

To get to those places, you have to go through a sort of death. For most of us, a marriage or committed relationship is the best hope we have of doing that. That's why marriage is such a beautiful ordeal. It's an ordeal in that it's a long, arduous road that will require you to give and give up quite a bit. It's beautiful because when you can do that, the rewards and pleasures are amazing. You'll feel more centered and more trusting of yourself and your partner.

You'll be able to deal with relationship conflict more effectively. And you'll be a lot less lonely and self-absorbed and a lot more happy and tuned in to the world around you.

So let me ask you again: Which marriage are you on with your current partner? And how many more do you think are still yet to come? May you find the courage, connection, and skillfulness to navigate through the many cycles of a long, loving relationship.

NOTE

1. Jung, C. G. Cited in E. E. Edinger, *Encounter with the Self: A Jungian Commentary on William Blake's "Illustration of the Book of Job."* Toronto: Inner City Books, 1986, p. 9.

The Sacredness of a Marriage

A Personal Reflection

Rita M. DeMaria

Our capacity to love is one of our inherent birthrights. As one of our biologically based, pleasurable emotions, love can be expressed sexually, emotionally, intellectually, and spiritually. No wonder there is so much mystery surrounding this complex emotion.

Just how do our biological needs connect with our spiritual needs? Part of the explanation comes from the fact that falling in love activates our inborn nature to bond with another human being. When the spark of love is kept alive and nurtured by the combined processes of bonding, shared experience, and sensual pleasure, the spark has the potential to become an eternal flame.

The romantic spark we call falling in love is a physical, emotional, psychological, and spiritual event. With this spark—some call it love; some call it lust—a relationship is vital and has the energy to grow and evolve. Without this spark, no couples that I know of have been able to revitalize their relationship when it was in trouble. Affection and passion are keys to the most successful intimate relationships. And its sexual expression is a powerful reinforcement. With all its ebbs and flows, romantic love can ignite a process that evolves from lust to reverence to sacredness.

A sacred marriage is fostered through a formula that combines chance, chemistry, bonding, choice, and commitment. The process begins when a chance meeting of two human beings triggers our biologically based emotional system to seek the satisfaction of our need for bonding, which is a basic need for attachment and connection. In an intimate relationship, these bonding needs are expressed and sustained through both affection and passion.

Romantic love has its taproot in our biology, but our psychological and emotional make-up determines the goodness-of-fit between two people. Those who fall in love never lose that loving feeling; it only fades for lack of nurturing. That is, many people just don't know how to nurture and rejuvenate their bond and reignite their spark. Knowledge, skill, and good will can reset the path of a neglected, short-circuited, or even damaged intimate relationship. Like a fire

Like a fire whose embers are waning, love must be continuously fed in order to raise the intensity of desire.

whose embers are waning, love must be continuously fed in order to raise the intensity of desire.

I cannot easily separate my clinical and personal experience of love. My personal experience colors and influences every aspect of my understanding about love. Although I have read and researched everything I can find about love and passion, my professional training never addressed how to help couples nurture or rekindle the spark in their relationships. Because I grew up in a family riddled with serious social, emotional, and psychological difficulties, the odds were against me from the start. My attitudes, emotions, and behaviors often reflected these influences in my interactions with my husband. In my marriage, we have been through some very low times—so low that at those moments going our separate ways seemed the only reasonable and sane option.

But there was that spark—and the unshakable bond that came from twenty-eight years of shared history. After twenty-one years of marriage, I am more in love than ever with my husband. I feel more grown up, sensuous, assertive, responsible, and creative than I believe I have ever felt before. I am also more vulnerable, more dependent, more open, and more trusting than I have ever been before. How did we get there with all the struggles in our relationship?

The answer is of course different for every couple, but for us I think it had something to do with the spark that did not die because of the bonding that we shared and that sustained us, even through our difficult times. Bonding fostered a pervasive, loving memory that has held us together and fueled our interest and excitement in being together—in love. I now feel blessed to be in this marriage with this man. We have woven a tapestry of life and love that has shaped each of us for the better. I love who I am now, and I love who he is now. The spark is deeper, wiser, and more vital. Our challenges just gave us many more rough edges to soften and new places to explore.

But I have wondered: "Am I lucky? Did I just pick the right person?" Or having been in the profession for many years, "Do I just know the skills?" I believe that our bond of affection and passion, cultivated through many years of respect and appreciation for both our children and ourselves, has cushioned us. The strength of our relationship (sparked initially by chance and chemistry and fortified by bonding and passion) allowed us be vulnerable with each other over time. Perhaps it's luck or perhaps it's skill. I choose to view it as faith—in our shared history and the strength of the bond that has evolved. Indeed, the capacity to be vulnerable with another person expands as emotional maturity evolves. Although our backgrounds and personalities may have shaped our initial responses to one another, over time our ability to be vulnerable allowed us to learn about ourselves and each other. Looking back, I see how we began with what might be called a fantasy of who the other person was—someone

The physical elements of love—the spark, the chemistry, and ultimately the bond—are essential ingredients if a couple hopes to complete their sacred journey together.

who we each wished would fulfill unmet needs and make up for past hurts. Where we arrived, however, was at a deeper and more realistic place of understanding, vulnerability, and respect that could only be achieved through the complexity of a loving, evolving marriage. We didn't find our soul mate; we became soul mates.

The beginning of love is a chance occurrence. The process of loving, however, is a challenge, a commitment, and a choice. There are highs and lows along the way for everyone, and there is no skipping lightly through the process. The physical elements of love—the spark, the chemistry, and ultimately the bond—are essential ingredients if a couple hopes to complete their sacred journey together. No matter what their level of distress, I believe that couples who are bonded physically, sexually, emotionally, and intellectually will have grave difficulties ending their marriage if it should falter. With knowledge, skills, and commitment, couples can move beyond the chemistry of lust and fantasy to the universal acceptance of oneself and the other.

This is the sacredness of marriage, a place of affection, passion, and reverence, which comes from consciously experiencing life and pleasure together as unique individuals.

A SHMILY for You

Gary Smalley, Greg Smalley, and Michael Smalley

What is it that keeps love passionate to the end? What secret must we unveil to keep romance alive? Surely it is something so powerful that most of us, no matter how hard we try, will never ascertain it. It must be so magical that only the couples who find their true soul mate can unleash its mighty power.

Maybe this is so, but we found a story that we think might hold the answer; in fact, it could be the potion for a happily-ever-after marriage. This is the end of our commentary. The answer is for you to discover. We fear that saying anything after this story might take away some nugget of truth that you need to make your love life the most satisfying adventure of all.

My grandparents were married for over half a century and played their own special game from the time they met. The goal of their game was to write the word *SHMILY* in a surprise place for the other to find. They took turns leaving SHMILY around the house, and as soon as one of them discovered it, it was that person's turn to hide it once more. They dragged SHMILY with their fingers through the sugar and flour containers to await whoever was preparing the next meal. They smeared it in the dew on the windows overlooking the patio where my grandma always fed us warm, homemade pudding with blue food coloring. SHMILY was written in the steam left on the mirror after a hot shower, where it would reappear, bath after bath. At one point my grandmother unrolled an entire roll of toilet paper to leave SHMILY on the very last sheet.

What is it that keeps love passionate to the end?

There was no end to the places SHMILY would pop up. Little notes with SHMILY scribbled hurriedly were found on dashboards and car seats, or taped to steering wheels—the notes stuffed inside shoes and left under pillows. SHMILY was written in the dust on the mantel and traced in the ashes of the fireplace. This mysterious word was as much a part of my grandparents' house as the furniture.

It took me a long time before I was able to fully appreciate my grandparents' game. Skepticism has kept me from believing in true love—one that is pure and enduring. However, I never doubted my grandparents' relationship.

They had love down pat. It was more than their flirtatious little games; it was a way of life. Their relationship was based on a devotion and passionate affection that not everyone is lucky enough to experience. Grandma and Grandpa held hands every chance they could. They stole kisses as they bumped into each other in their tiny kitchen. They finished each other's sentences and shared the daily crossword puzzle and word jumble. My grandma whispered to me about how cute my grandpa was, how handsome and old he had grown to be. She claimed that she really knew "how to pick 'em." Before every meal they bowed their heads and gave thanks, marveling at their blessings: a wonderful family, good fortune, and each other.

They had love down pat. It was more than their flirtatious little games; it was a way of life.

But there was a dark cloud in my grandparents' life: my grandmother had breast cancer. The disease had first appeared ten years earlier. As always, Grandpa was with her every step of the way. He comforted her in their yellow room, painted that way so that she could always be surrounded by sunshine, even when she was too sick to go outside. Now the cancer was again attacking her body. With the help of a cane and my grandpa's steady hand, they went to church every morning. But my grandma grew steadily weaker until, finally, she could not leave the house anymore. For a while Grandpa would go to church alone, praying to God to watch over his wife.

Then one day, what we all dreaded finally happened: Grandma was gone. SHMILY—it was scrawled in yellow on the pink ribbons of my grandma's funeral bouquet. As the crowd thinned and the last mourners turned to leave, aunts, uncles, cousins, and other family members came forward and gathered around Grandma one last time. Grandpa stepped up to my grandmother's casket and, taking a shaky breath, he began to sing to her. Through his tears and grief the song came, a deep and throaty lullaby. Shaking with my own sorrow, I will never forget that moment. For I knew that, although I couldn't begin to fathom the depth of their love, I had been privileged to witness its unmatched beauty.

S-H-M-I-L-Y: See How Much I Love You.

—Author Unknown

The Magic of Older Love

Stoking Your Marital Fires Through the Years

Claudia Arp and David Arp

Young love is a flame; very pretty, very hot and fierce, but still only light and flickering. The love of the older and disciplined heart is as coals, deep-burning, unquenchable.—Henry Ward Beecher

Oh, the wonderful comfort of being totally accepted and loved. Sacred marriage history: years of living filled with joy, grace, laughter, hurts, forgiveness. Shared memories no one else can enter. Sunrise. Sunset. Joined together in the rhythm of love and life. Two before the fire. Eyes meet and

Keeping the Magic Alive

1. Be playful: Loosen up and look for romance. Remember, getting there is half the fun.

speak their own private language of love. Hands held through the years. A seasoned marriage passes the test of time—and endures. This is marriage magic at its best!

Marriage magic that lasts through the years is coveted by the young, achieved by the fortunate, envied by all. How much is luck? How much is magic? How much is work? We would agree that luck, magic, and chemistry play a role. We still remember the early days of our love—how every waking moment was focused on wanting to be together, to be close, to hold hands, kiss, and dream of a lifetime of love together. Then wedding bells. Reality. Children. Three very active boys. Careers. Life happens and where does the magic go? Can it be revived? Yes, but it takes more than magic. It takes work; it takes time. But for the brave who are willing to work and pursue it, marriage magic in older, seasoned relationships can be the best yet.

Mature Marriage Magic

"We just celebrated our fifty-sixth wedding anniversary," Martha, a participant in one of our seminars, said. "It may sound a little hokey, but on the way home from our anniversary dinner, we sang our old favorite songs to each other. You know, songs like, 'Let me call you Sweetheart, I'm in love with you.' "

We looked at each other. This couple *still* has the magic. Then we began to wonder if we will still be singing to each other after we have been married fifty-six years. Will you? Perhaps, but only if you—and we—don't take the magic for granted and only if we keep nurturing our relationship with fun, laughter, romance, and other healthy habits.

Keeping the Magic Alive

2. Be affectionate: Take time to cuddle, laugh, hold hands, and share intimate thoughts.

Love and intimacy in a marriage grow by stages, but if ignored at any stage the flame of love and romance can grow dim or even go out. A fulfilling and enjoyable love life can add much pleasure to the second half of marriage, especially if you keep the magic alive.

Rekindle the Magic

We are convinced that you can stoke your own marital fire and enhance the kind of love you will achieve in the future as you go through the various stages of marriage. Perhaps the best time to nurture older love is when you are young. A secret of keeping love alive when the children arrive is making sure that you keep investing in your own love life. From our observations most parents of young children are stressed out and sleep deprived. But during these hectic parenting years, little acts of thoughtfulness to keep love alive—making time for dating and planning short but romantic getaways or always kissing when you say hello and good-bye—will keep the magic from totally disappearing.

Keeping the Magic Alive

3. Be in shape: Stay fit mentally and physically.

The Joy of Older Love

From working with older marriages we know that when the kids leave home romance can be rekindled. But often other factors come into play. For years in our own relationship we looked forward to the extra freedom and flexibility we would have in our love life when our last child left home. And although we weren't totally disappointed, we had not counted on bad backs or other things like work deadlines that seemed to multiply. We still had to work at the "magic" part of love, but it has been well worth it. From our own experience, older love is the best.

The Facets of Older Love

A couple's love life over the years is like a multifaceted diamond. Older love highlights different facets than younger love, such as *trust*. The trust that develops over the years of a relationship gives a deeper sense of feeling safe with each other. So you have a few extra pounds or response time is longer—not to worry—at this stage your love life can be a romantic stroll—not a hectic sprint! Now you can claim time for romance. Time for magic. Time for loving someone you trust completely.

The second facet of older love is *mutuality*—freely choosing to love each other over the years, knowing that each partner wants to be in this relationship. The history of growing and adapting to each other's changing needs over the years adds a dimension to love that young lovers can never know.

Honesty is the third facet of mature love. Openly communicating your true feelings with each other over the years lays the foundation for openness and honesty in your love life. Honesty is as necessary to a healthy love life as sunlight is to flowers and trees. Think of young love as a small oak sprig, planted with great hope of future growth. Now picture old love as a towering oak tree, strong and secure, protecting your relationship. That's the difference in young and old love.

The fourth facet of older love is *intimacy*—being soul mates and feeling close over the years. Intimacy is the intangible quality of unity and understanding and synergy that over the years moves a relationship from acquaintance or friend to lover and soul mate. Intimacy allows you to share your dreams, needs, fears, and desires. Intimacy deepens as the years go by.

The fifth facet, *pleasure,* increases with each year of loving each other. Giving joy and comfort includes the act of making love but also includes touching and holding hands, spontaneous cuddles, hugs and kisses, rubbing your lover's aching foot or leg, sharing a tradition of a daily tea time for two over many years, or sitting alone on the porch swing without saying a word. All these are pleasures of older love.

The last facet of older love is *sex*. Joining together physically and loving each other is one of the rewards of love in the second

Keeping the Magic Alive

4. Be adventuresome: Take some risks. Try a little spontaneity.

half of life. David and Vera Mace, pioneers in marriage education wrote in their book, *Letters to a Retired Couple*,[1] that in the latter years the sexual relationship is not so much a matter of performance as it is the expression of a warm and close love relationship.

Understanding the facets of older love—trust, mutuality, honesty, intimacy, pleasure, and sex—will help you create your own diamond-studded love life. Far from being the "left-over," older love can truly be the dessert! Let us encourage you. Go on and take the risk. Stoke your own fire and experience the joys of older love. As Robert Browning so eloquently expressed, "The best is yet to be!"

NOTE

1. Mace, D., and Mace, V. *Letters to a Retired Couple.* Valley Forge, Penn.: Judson, 1985.

Love the Second Time Around

Emily B. Visher and John S. Visher

Love and marriage the first time around is an all-consuming, gloriously expansive emotion that sweeps through the individuals and carries them along through the marriage, the honeymoon, and beyond. Through the months and years ahead the intensity of that love diminishes, and many begin to take the relationship for granted. If love is not nourished it erodes and slowly fades away.

Love and marriage the second time around is also an all-consuming, glorious, emotion. However, for many couples with children, the expansiveness of first love is missing, and even the marriage is a bittersweet experience. The honeymoon, if there is one, is often short-lived and is followed by a period in which the couple's intimacy is squeezed into very precious moments the two manage to have alone. As one remarried mother told us, "There's a big difference between a first and second marriage. In my first wedding everyone was happy. When I remarried everyone was crying. We didn't have a honeymoon because of all the children, and that first night my daughter came into our bedroom and said, 'I don't feel well,' at which point she proceeded to throw up all over the bed."

Many couples in first marriages find their love closing in and closing down, whereas those in second marriages find their love becoming deeper and sweeter as the years go by. Their honeymoon years come not at the beginning as in first marriages but later on during the so-called empty nest period. In other words, over time the expansiveness of love in first marriages frequently contracts and becomes more constricted; in subsequent marriages the reverse occurs. The internal and external restraints become loosened, and love is free to expand and be fully experienced.

For many years we have focused our attention on love the second time around, and although it is true that every couple's story is unique, it is also true that universal themes emerge in the experience of loving in the context of an instant family. From our connections with remarried parents and stepparents, we believe the scenarios we describe next are common.

We have found that for most couples, previous marriages have a profound effect on the new relationships. For some, the excitement and emotional pull of falling in love again is actually more intense than it was the first time, whereas others find themselves withholding emotionally because they cannot believe that the relationship will develop into something permanent. Trust is essential for loving relationships, and after a divorce many people's loss of trust inhibits their ability to fall in love again. It takes time to restore their faith and trust in the future. As one remarried father said, "I tried to reassure myself that what was happening between us wouldn't slip away, but I wasn't sure for a very long time whether or not my future wife's feelings for me were temporary. My love for her built over a long time as I gained more trust."

Lessons learned in first marriages can bring new self-knowledge and self-awareness that can benefit new love relationships.

This awareness can help those who love the second time around because the passions of their hearts are then tempered by new wisdom in their heads. Individuals frequently tell us that they were naïve in their original understandings of how to make a marriage work. They say that they have now learned that it takes work to sustain a good marital relationship, that tolerance and acceptance are necessary to make intimate relationships survive, and that all of their desires will not be fulfilled by their partner. Others describe different contributions from their new awareness. For example, some people feel strongly that if their *head* tells them that a relationship will not work out well, they should end it—or perhaps not even *begin* it—even though that might be very difficult.

Lessons learned in first marriages can bring new self-knowledge and self-awareness that can benefit new love relationships.

Learning from previous marriage experiences can also help people guard against repeating old patterns in their new marriages. One remarried woman clearly illustrated this point when she said, "I was beginning to fall into similar patterns as I had in my first marriage. I had learned that they didn't work in relationships, and I realized what was happening. I said to myself, 'I'm not going to do it; we've got to get out of this pattern. And we did.'" In essence, in second marriages many individuals have the cognitive ability to avoid doing what they did that previously led to negative consequences.

Probably the greatest influence exerted from previous marriages involves the legacy of children. Much as parents adore them, they often severely underestimate the emotional complexity and initial chaos they will experience because of the existence of children. For a period of time the two adults are never alone. Even when they are, the emotional tangles in dealing with the children keep pulling at them.

Some of these struggles are internal. Parents without custody may feel guilty about their connection (or lack of connection) with their children, and new stepparents may feel considerable anxiety about being rejected by their stepchildren.

The husband may think, "I am so tied to my kids, and I feel very guilty that I am abandoning them. They are very angry at me, and I worry about what is going to happen to them, and I hope their anger won't be permanent."

Michelle Pfeiffer and David Kelley

MICHELLE: It just keeps getting better. Because we weren't kids when we got together, we're much more realistic about what we expect. I think when we met, we were each formed. We knew who we were, and we knew what we wanted.

—*McCall's,* November 1999

The wife may think, "Fortunately for me, my children are with me and I don't have that same feeling of abandoning them. Even so, when we got married it seemed almost overwhelming to think of all the obstacles and hurdles, though we didn't actually anticipate what they *really* would be. I hadn't expected to be met with rejection from my stepchildren, and I feel very anxious a lot of the time."

Love that is fraught with the guilt and anxiety so apparent in these thoughts lacks the essential sense of freedom and spontaneity necessary to healthy relationships.

Interactional struggles also arise due to the necessity of developing new relationships while living closely with individuals who do not know one another very well. These internal conflicts and the highly charged interpersonal family atmosphere test the couple's strength of love and commitment from the very day they are married.

It may be easy to fall in love the second time around, but when children are involved, allowing this love to develop and blossom into a sustaining relationship can be a painful challenge. During these early months of chaos the wife just quoted had an image flash

Because of previous losses, in successful remarriages there is often a poignancy in the depth and awareness of love.

repeatedly into her consciousness in which she and her husband were on either side of a huge abyss, reaching out in an attempt to touch each other and being pulled apart by the arms and hands of the children.

Remarried couples hunger for solitary, intimate times; they snatch what moments they can. But for most it is only when they are geographically far from home that they can let go of their identity as parents. In the words of one couple, "When we are away we feel free! Our spirits soar and our deepest loving is released! There are few tensions and little anxiety, and we enjoy the fun and intimacy in our relationship without the scrutiny and emotional responses of our children. These times replenish our souls and bring the depth of our love into full consciousness." Maintaining a loving relationship in the midst of early stepfamily chaos is anything but easy. However, because couples often cannot readily get away together, they often find that dealing with the challenges *together* hastens rather than hinders the development of a strong and loving relationship.

Most couples need to let go of their original expectations and understand that their new family requires a different map from the one they have in their heads. Unfortunately, some couples have difficulty keeping the long-term picture in mind, and even though they may still love each other, the complexity of the situation pushes them apart. They must be willing to work together to achieve long-term goals.

There are not, of course, any easy and quick solutions. However, when the adults support each other, over the years the family settles down and the joy in their couple relationship keeps growing and expanding. In remarriages, the couple relationship is uniquely tested and can grow strong and constant from working together to meet the many family challenges. Partners frequently express a conscious and continuing appreciation and thankfulness for the love they are experiencing the second time around.

These relationships are very special.

Since Seventh Grade

John Fiske and Martie Fiske

MARTIE: We talked until we fell in love, waiting on those uncomfy brick steps of our high school for that big clunky school bus.

JOHN: I picked you out because you were good-looking and laughed at my jokes. You even expressed occasional interest in me, which felt phenomenal. We talked about everything. You came from an analytical family and discussed things. My two brothers and I just did stuff.

MARTIE: And you were pretty cute, too, even if your ears did stick out. You were also the first person I knew who wasn't any kind of a snob. That was enthralling, because I could tell that you enjoyed more people that way. I wanted to be like that.

JOHN: We were both in Mrs. Elting's class, too. Remember that debate when I argued that the Romans were superior to the Greeks, and you explained why the Greeks were better than the Romans. I of course won. But you claimed triumph, in part because you were right and also because you cited specifics—something to do with a safety pin.

JOHN: So it wasn't just your gorgeous body, it was also your curious brain.

MARTIE: And even though I know I'm not gorgeous or brilliant, I suspect I am still susceptible to your persistent, possibly sincere flattery.

MARTIE: Now there you go doing your "peacemaker" bit and diffusing every contest with humor. You have a compulsion to see every situation as a win-win deal. That revelation—that you could view conflict as fun for everybody—snagged my heartstrings. And often drove me bananas! I liked a good argument and still consider it healthy.

JOHN: But that debate shows that I was also taken by your brain, and you made it easy for me not to resent your being smart. You said interesting things. You didn't lord it over people. You're a born teacher, and you often talk about something intriguing to you in a way that makes it intriguing to me. So it wasn't just your gorgeous body; it was also your curious brain.

MARTIE: And even though I know I'm not gorgeous or brilliant, I suspect I am still susceptible to your persistent, possibly sincere flattery.

JOHN: It's not flattery! We agreed early on that the only way our relationship would survive would be if we each were totally open and honest with one another. Over the years, that principle has served us well.

MARTIE: So I don't have to praise your crummy carpentry but must say that I revere you as the best possible grandfather. Along with honesty we vowed equality, even as teeny-boppers in those reeking patriarchal late 1940s. Since I was then a bit taller than you—I could even beat you in football—our partnership was a natural ground rule that has endured well past your gaining several good-looking inches on me.

JOHN: So is it the early respect we promised each other? Always listening intently, assuming validity in the other's positions? I guess that's what makes it possible for me to buy stocks and you to buy treasuries.

MARTIE: I also think as kids we became enthralled by the strangeness of what the other had to confess, with the novelty of the other's often-stunning concerns. Like you could get all bug-eyed over sports, and I had a duty to understand why. And you were the first to listen to me talk about my deadly depressions. That made for a kind of partnership, right there, maintained by talk, by telling, by explaining, by admitting, and by negotiating.

JOHN: Almost from the beginning I felt a magnetism or need to be with you and a hole or hiatus if you were not there. This usually occurred when something was happening that I thought you would enjoy, whether reading a good book or seeing ducks squabbling in the river. I could talk with you about poetry, art, music, or beauty in many forms, and there was no one else who would listen the way you did or respond in some fascinating way as you did. I just wanted to be with you because I enjoyed so much anything we did together.

Also, I think part of our success as a couple was based on the early respect we promised each other. We always listened intently to each other, assuming validity in the other's thoughts. You would correct me and I knew you were right—at least some of the time. You also acknowledged, over and over, how much I was teaching you. We do not take each other for granted and often repeat how much we value the other.

MARTIE: Ahhh. You are also revealing an essential commitment to the relationship, an assumption of togetherness that came for both of us with our wedding vows, which in an avant garde kind of way we memorized. We shared a compulsion to be pure and original. If we hadn't both come from families who considered marriage inviolable, we wouldn't have survived some terrible times. You're such an optimist you can hardly admit these ugly chapters in our past.

But we did not even conceive of divorce during our decade of desperation, raising three babies, always feeling broke, restless in our jobs or lack thereof, and without the consolation of therapy, drugs, helping family, or other support. We did crazy, outrageously ambitious stuff like taking our three kids, dog, and a cousin cross-country camping. And I imagined that razor blades might deliver me from my convictions of inadequacy.

Tom Hanks and Rita Wilson

TOM: I am standing here because the woman I share my life with has taught me and demonstrates to me every day just what love is.

—Academy Award acceptance speech, 1994

JOHN: I knew things were hard. I was around as much as I could be and saw a lot of tension at times. We were both on edge. There were raised voices in the house a lot, certainly more than I wanted. I did not know how desperate, depressed, despondent you were about raising children, not having a "real" job—all those early feminist issues.

I should have done something, or a number of things, in response. But I always had this inner confidence in you and your own strength, that you would manage and come through fine. Probably part of my love for you is this admiration of your inner strength. You still have it, and I still am awed by it: your sense of commitment, determination, discipline, duty, energy, integrity. You do your jobs so well.

Let me not to the marriage of true minds
Admit impediments. Love is not love
Which alters when it alteration finds,
Or bends with the remover to remove:
O, no! it is an ever-fixed mark . . .

—William Shakespeare, Sonnet 116

Our relationship thrives because we are completely committed to each other, enjoy each other's company, and want to spend time doing things together. "Love is not love/Which alters when it alteration finds," and we have ridden this commitment through sickness and health, poor and rich. "O, no! it is an ever-fixed mark." We have been guided by that.

When you get all dressed up and stand in front of all your family and friends in church and say you are forever going to see each other through thick and thin, good and bad, for richer or for poorer, that's commitment, and when someone does that for you it means something.

Martie: Earlier I said I wanted to be a non-snob like you. Other qualities magnetized me: your ease and joy with your body, your utterly original and mesmerizing whimsy, your intoxication with me from which you have yet to recover, the rich archives of your brain. I guess I wanted all that in my treasure house. So I stayed loyal to the best friend I ever had.

Reflections on True Love

W. Kim Halford

The night my father died it was very hot and humid. It was the sort of night that would have been difficult to sleep through anyway.

Two weeks before that night, my sister rang about ten o'clock at night. My father had been moved to intensive care. Throughout the months of his current hospital admission we had been told that his lung problems (he had emphysema) were not life threatening. The doctors had said his condition should stabilize, and then he would be able to return home to my mother. Now it seemed something more serious was wrong. "It might be better if you come to Melbourne, just in case."

I told my wife, Barbara, the news. I booked the thousand-mile flight to Melbourne for early the next morning. We went to bed. I felt tired but did not fall asleep. Half-formed ideas flickered in my head. Should I get up and ring the doctor to find out what was going on? Was this yet another health scare for my father, or was he going to die?

Barbara was half asleep but seemed to sense my restlessness. Her arm curled round me, drew me close. She murmured gently. I must have drifted off to sleep, as I next saw the pink of early morning, visible through the window.

For the next ten days I lived with my mother. Each day we drove to the hospital in the city. My father lay semiconscious in intensive care, tubes and monitors plugged into him. I stroked his brow, talked to him. Mum and I spoke in hushed tones and watched his chest labor up and down. We spoke to endless streams of men and women in white coats. They spoke gravely in concerned tones before hurrying away.

In the evenings I cooked elaborate meals for my mother and me. Sometimes we went out for dinner—anything to distract us from the pain of the hospital visits.

Each night I rang Barbara. I told her the details of the hospital visit, described how my Mum was going. She listened 'til I was exhausted of things to say. Then we talked about our young sons, James and Chris, and about their day. Barbara told me about her day. The conversations provided some normality to cling to.

After ten days of visits my father seemed to be recovering. Although still semiconscious he was to be transferred out of intensive care. My wife, my sons, and my job beckoned me. My employer had been supportive, but I had missed nearly two weeks of work. This was not the first time I had taken time off work to be with my father during a health crisis. So I flew home.

Three nights later the telephone rang. It was my sister Sue again. Dad had died. Sue told me details of what happened. We probably spoke about some other things, almost certainly about my trip back to Melbourne for the funeral. But when I tried to relay my conversation to Barbara I could not remember anything other than that Dad had died.

The night my father died it was hot and humid. It was the sort of night that would have been difficult to sleep anyway. But I was feeling agitated, wound up, numb. I thought jerky, disconnected thoughts. I felt a sadness so intense it hurt.

Barbara curled up next to me on the sofa. She stroked me gently on the back and neck—the way she has countless times when I am tense or tired, except the touch was so gentle this time. I talked a little, but not much. Eventually a fitful sleep came. In the dark hours of that evening I was not alone. I was loved.

Now that I am middle aged, I do not mistake the excitement of lust for true love.

When I was a young man I thought love was that passion, lust, exhilaration that can overwhelm when you are besotted with someone. I

In fact, I no longer believe that people fall in love.

still think that is an exciting feeling—a feeling that should be savored. But now that I am middle aged, I do not mistake the excitement of lust for true love.

In fact, I no longer believe that people fall in love. People fall into lust and they fall into attraction, which are exciting. But lust is not love, and love is not something you fall into. Two mutually besotted people who just met can know great passion, but they cannot know the depth of love of a couple who have shared a lifetime together.

I think true love is built across a lifetime. Initial attraction is built into love through sharing births, deaths, marriages, friendships, celebrations, mourning, and the mundane. In my research on couples, my practice as a couple therapist, and in my life, it is the long-term sharing of the journey of life that I see as love. That is the love people tell me they seek.

Initial attraction is important, but it is the commitment and the sharing over time that develops love. So what determines if a couple stays together and builds a loving relationship? Many things determine relationship outcome: the culture in which one is raised, the support of family and friends, relationship skills like communication and conflict management, and the ability of each partner to manage stress. Good luck also helps. Good luck provides a mix of joys to share and manageable challenges to overcome for the couple.

I think true love is built across a lifetime.

Finding the right partner is much overemphasized in love. We each are capable of loving many other people as life partners. Chance determines whom we meet. Love may be built when we seize the opportunity to build a relationship with someone to whom we are attracted. If we do what we can to build love, and if the roll of the cosmic dice favors us, then we may be rewarded with true love.

Flavors of Love

Wayne M. Sotile and Mary O. Sotile

f you had asked us ten years ago what love's got to do with marriage, we would have answered with the confidence and certainty of seasoned marriage counselors. First we would have recited a list of "don'ts"—things you must avoid to protect your love:

- Don't be unfaithful, either in actions or words.
- Don't be abusive.
- Don't let your self-focused notions of love ruin your communication, friendship, or romance.

Next, with the pseudo-wisdom that comes from diligent academic study, we would have cautioned that being "in love" is the same as being infatuated and is aided by a hormonal and brain-chemical concoction that intoxicates you and blurs your vision. Unfortunately, we'd caution, this flavor of love won't last. Eventually your preoccupying passion for each other will quiet. The perceptions, role divisions, and relationship dances borne of infatuation feel good for only a short while. Be prepared, we would have urged you, to periodically renegotiate your roles and change your dances or your love will die.

We still believe that certain mistakes can kill any relationship. And we still caution our clients that the buzz of infatuation is relatively brief. But we also revel in helping couples have faith that a lifelong marriage marinates into ever-changing flavors of love. How does this happen? Our own journey and our experiences as marriage counselors to over six thousand couples have left us skeptical that *any* set of guidelines or concepts can fully answer this question. Certainly nothing we've ever read or written can truly account for the happiness and excitement we still feel (after twenty-two years of marriage) when we are together or for the loss we feel when we are apart. But even though we've lost our academic clarity, we've gained what feels like a wisdom known only in the hearts of those who have loved each other for decades. We can sum it up this way: *falling in love is easy, but staying in love is about heroism; it's about creating safe spaces for each other.*

We have always known that we were in love. Here are some general points, as well as illustrations from our own letters, that show the varying flavors of our love for each other.

You know you're in love when . . . your deepest dreams stir similar dreams in your partner.

Dear Mary,
I love to remember our second date, when we talked through the night, fantasizing about getting married and, someday, having two brown-haired daughters.

You know you're in love when . . . being together stirs your favorite masculine or feminine feelings.

Dear Mary,
I love how you make me feel strong, never ashamed or blamed, even when I'm scared or when I feel that I have failed. I love how you admire me, even when I don't admire myself. I love how you thank me, even when I feel that I haven't given enough.

You know you're in love when . . . you are willing to stretch beyond your heart-felt limitations if that's what it takes to protect your partner.

Dear Mary,
It still touches my heart when I recall how generously and tenderly you cared for me when I burned my leg in that tractor accident. I know how squeamish you are. Yet you nursed my leg—every day, many times every day. You never hesitated; you never complained. At the time I was in too much pain to even notice your heroics. But I remember. And I will never forget how vulnerable I felt and that no one ever before took such selfless care of me.

You know you're in love when . . . your partner's responses stretch you to take better care of yourself than you feel you deserve.

> Dear Mary,
> Thank you for helping me learn how to play and for playing with me. Thank you for so often reminding me as we say goodbye, "Take time on this trip to relax; don't just work every night in your hotel room." Thank you for teaching me that I deserved to create my own version of Christmas holidays.

You know you're in love when . . . your relationship is the safest place you can imagine when you're afraid or vulnerable.

> Dear Mary,
> Thank you for making our marriage the same sort of safe space for me that my relationships with each of my grandparents always were. You are my new hero.

You know you're in love when . . . your newest set of deepest dreams stir similar dreams in your partner.

> Dear Mary,
> These days, I love fantasizing with you about how, maybe one day, our beautiful Rebecca and Julia will be having our brown-haired grandbabies. In the meantime, I sure am enjoying dancing with you in our empty nest!

Finally, and most important, ***you know you'll stay in love when*** . . . you've grown to appreciate your different ways of loving each other.

Dear Wayne,

I read your letters to me with a complex mixture of emotion. The primary feeling is one of joy at my good fortune. I am loved by a wonderful person who demonstrates his love for me with such straightforward beauty and poetry.

A second feeling, though, is one of inadequacy because I am not a poet. What you express boldly and beautifully in word and deed, I demonstrate quietly and subtly. You grew up in a family that daily sings its love for each other to the rafters while my family awkwardly whispers those sentiments—and only occasionally. Both families love deeply but it looks so different.

Thank you, Wayne, for knowing that still waters often do run deep, for letting the quiet ways I most comfortably and naturally show my love for you count. Thank you also for your patience, as I've learned to express my love in ways that are easier for you to see and hear.

I love you with my life,

Mary

Romantic love comes in many flavors and expressions. Some are better condensed into words than others. Some soar like a symphony while others hum along like a catchy tune. Some jump up and applaud while others sit back and smile.

It is a good day when we can generously express our love in the ways our partner most appreciates. It is also a good day when we can graciously accept what our partner offers as an expression of love, even when it's not our first choice. This is the glue that makes a resilient love relationship, and a loving relationship is our best chance for safe passage through the journey of life.

A Love Letter to My Wife After 65 Years

Art Linkletter

Dear Lois:

For me it was not love at first sight. In fact, I thought I'd try to get a dance with you at my annual fraternity party just to snatch you away from my favorite fraternity brother, "Pigeon."

You see, I had a reputation around San Diego State College for stealing Allen Flavin's dates at each and every Tau Delta Chi dance. This night was to be no exception. Or so I thought.

To begin with he refused to introduce me. Then he refused to let me cut in on him during a dreamy waltz.

Then when I finally secured your phone number from one of your friends, you turned me down cold over the phone, explaining that your mother didn't let you go out with anyone she hadn't met . . . and especially not college boys trolling for dates with young high school girls.

"What!" I exclaimed, "You're a high schooler? With that gorgeous sequin jacket and beautiful legs I saw dancing around at the party. . . . This I've got to see again. Put your mother on the phone!"

Twenty minutes later, using the same techniques that I later used to scale the peaks of radio and TV, I had a date for dinner at your house under the watchful eye of Mama.

It was a gorgeous dinner and I would have come back again, even if you hadn't turned out to be the best dancer I ever clutched to my bosom. However, in the next year we wore out several of the best rugs in your living room and I gained fifteen pounds.

Your brunette beauty, lovely smile, and kissable lips eliminated any prejudice I might have had about going with a mere twelfth grader. After all, I was a junior in college, the president of the Men Students, and captain of the basketball team. I was fairly certain that I was, indeed, a true big shot on the campus with my choice of the queens.

Most of your friends thought it would never last. We were so different in our backgrounds and personalities. I was the first orphan, the first Canadian, and the first ex-hobo you had ever met.

I remember you listening to me, wide-eyed, as I told you about my experiences between high school and college riding freight trains across the Rockies, sleeping in YMCA gyms, working as a bus boy in a night club, hanging up hot livers freshly killed in the offal room of Armour's plant in St. Paul, graduating from freight cars to passenger trains as an upwardly mobile hobo, typing my way through the 1929 Wall Street crash in the bond department of the National City Bank of New York, standing in the crow's nest of the S.S. American Legion off the coast of Buenos Aires as a cadet-sailor—and finally returning to San Diego at eighteen to become an English teacher. It was a thrilling story for you, who had never been farther from home than Los Angeles, 120 miles away, and had always had a loving middle-class home to live in.

You never let on that you worried about my "worldly" knowledge or carnal experiences, and you never complained that I had little or no money, which necessitated our going to street dances and free carnivals, and entering dance contests at Mission Beach in order to get in for nothing. And your wonderful folks, Jack and Peg, never questioned my constantly changing sleeping quarters as I took various jobs as a "house boy" and gardener to get me through school.

We must have seemed the original odd couple, and the odds against our marriage reached astronomical proportions.

Yes, we must have seemed the original odd couple, and the odds against our marriage reached astronomical proportions.

A year and a half later, after I had graduated and become a temporary radio announcer at Station KGB and you had enrolled as a freshman at State, we almost parted.

Getting ready to start your sophomore year, I scoffed at your inexperience in the world and kidded you unmercifully about being a "home" girl who had never been anywhere or seen anything.

I bragged about all the things I had already done, while you were just a quiet little girl protected by a watchful Mama. You were quiet, reserved, and unadventurous. You had never even had a job. And finally I taunted you with the question, "Don't you ever wonder what's going on out there in the big world?"

Two weeks later, unannounced to me, you got on a bus with your mother and left for Tucson, Arizona. Without so much as a hint of your plans, you had enrolled at the University of Arizona, and I was waving goodbye with tears running down my cheeks. That was really my first inkling that there was something more than a sweet smile and an agreeable personality lurking behind those hazel eyes. I've never forgotten that experience in the sixty-five years that have passed since then, and I don't mind confessing that your swift action put a brake on my tongue forever.

I had lost you. Or so I thought, as the days went on.

And then your first letter arrived. My heart started beating again as I read your explanation of why you had to leave me that way. You *did* love me. You *were* going to return. And I *was* the only man in your heart.

In fact, I was so encouraged and uplifted by this good news that I immediately wrote a mushy love letter and included *your* letter with the misspelled words corrected. (You never could spell, you know.)

Ronald and Nancy Reagan

Ronald: God must think a lot of me to have given me you.

—*People Weekly,* February 1996, from his 1952 movie, *The Winning Team*

An eternity later (at Christmas time) you returned to tell me of your exciting life in Arizona, which included a tantalizing description of a certain football captain you had been seeing casually. You tried to comfort me, but I was far from comforted.

The following week we announced our engagement. And the following Thanksgiving we began the long and wonderful life together that has made me the happiest man in the world.

But life is what happens to you while you're making other plans. I'm sure that *you* planned, after we married, to raise a family and live happily forever after near your parents and friends in San Diego. I had a nice, permanent job as program director of KGB, and we would follow the conservative pattern of our peers.

Alas, I had other ambitions that I had failed to mention to you. My early odyssey to the outside world had opened my eyes to the bigger opportunities that beckoned far from our small town. In the next five years we moved eight times, and my career goals changed as often. I was hired, fired, promoted, rejected, catapulted to stardom, and then canceled. It was a wild yo-yo ride and, surprisingly, you went along with it, trusting completely in my judgment and never questioning the outcome.

Once again you surprised and delighted me with your spunk

and resolve. Along the way we had five children and traveled to Texas, San Francisco, and Hollywood and then back to San Francisco before settling permanently (I think) in Hollywood.

You provided the stability of a loving home base to which I could retreat at times from the jungle warfare of show business. You produced the warm, wonderful family of three girls and two boys that satisfied my hunger for a full family life that I had never known before.

Now in our eighties, with eight grandchildren and eleven great grandchildren, our life is still "happening." And I still have an appetite for change and adventure.

Perhaps we'll buy a boat and sail around the world. Or I'll accept another job as ambassador to some challenging foreign country. Or . . .

Now in our eighties, with eight grandchildren and eleven great grandchildren, our life is still "happening."

Wait and see. And be there with me!

MASTERY

The Birth of Love

Harville Hendrix

I will show you a love potion without drug or any witch's spell: if you wish to be loved, love.—Hecato

When we fall in love, suddenly we see life in technicolor. We nibble each other's ears and tell each other *everything;* our limitations and rigidities melt away. We're sexier, smarter, funnier, more giving. Now we feel whole; we feel like *ourselves;* we are connected.

But inevitably—whether we marry or move in together—things just start to go wrong. The veil of illusion falls away, and it seems that our partners are different than we thought they were. It turns out they have qualities that we can't bear. Even qualities we once admired grate on us. Old hurts are reactivated, as we realize that our partners cannot or will not love and care for us as they promised or as we hoped. Our dream shatters and we feel *disconnected.*

Disillusionment turns to anger. Because our partner no longer willingly gives us what we need, we change tactics, trying to coerce our partners into caring—through anger, crying, withdrawal, shame, intimidation, criticism—whatever works. The *power struggle* has begun and may go on for many years until we split or settle into an uneasy truce, or perhaps seek help—desperate to feel alive and whole again, to have our dream back and feel *reconnected.*

The Imago Emerges

What is going on here? My wife, Helen, and I, after reflecting deeply on this question, have come to this conclusion: if this happens to you, you have found an Imago (Ih-Mah-Go) partner—someone, we regret to say, *who is uniquely unqualified* (at the moment) to give you the love you want. Well, this is what's *supposed* to happen.

Let us explain. We all think that we have free choice when it comes to selecting our partners. But our primitive "old" brain has a compelling, non-negotiable drive to restore the feeling of aliveness, wholeness, and connectedness with which we came into the world. To accomplish this, it must repair the damage done in childhood as a result of needs not met, in a relationship with a person who resembles our caretakers.

You'd think, then, that we would choose someone who had what our caretakers lacked—and of course this is what we unconsciously seek. Would that it were so! But the old brain has a mind of its own, carrying its own image of the perfect partner, a complex synthesis of qualities formed in reaction to the way our caretakers responded to our needs. Every pleasure or pain, every transaction of childhood, has left its mark on us, and these collective impressions form an unconscious picture we're always trying to match up as we scan our environment for a suitable mate.

Try this:

Make a list of positive and negative traits of both your parents. Then make a similar list describing your partner. Compare.

This image of "the person who will join with me and make me whole again" we call the Imago.

Although we consciously seek only the positive traits, the negative traits of our caretakers are more indelibly imprinted in our Imago picture because those traits caused the wounds we now seek to heal. Paradoxically, our unconscious need is to have our feelings of aliveness and wholeness restored by someone with the same deficits of care and attention that hurt us in the first place.

So when we fall in love, our old brain is telling us that we've found someone with whom we can complete our unfinished childhood business, meet certain biological imperatives, and recover our wholeness. Our imperfect caretakers, "freeze dried" in the memories of childhood, are "reconstituted" in our partner. Unfortunately,

Check it out:

Make a list of the traits you like least in your partner. Then make a list of the traits you like best in yourself. Compare.

because we don't understand what's going on, we're shocked when the awful truth of our beloved surfaces.

But that's not all the bad news. Another powerful component of our Imago is that we also seek the qualities missing in ourselves—both good and bad—that got lost in the shuffle of socialization. If we are shy, we seek someone outgoing; if we're disorganized, we're attracted to someone cool and rational. The anger we repressed because it was punished in our home and that we unconsciously hate ourselves for feeling, we "annex" in our partner. But eventually, when our own feelings—our repressed exuberance or anger—are stirred, we are uncomfortable and criticize our partners for being *too* outgoing, *too* coldly rational, *too* temperamental.

Waking Up to Reality

All of this seems to be a recipe for disaster, and for a long time this depressing state of affairs puzzled us. How can we resolve our childhood issues if our partners wound us in the same ways as our caretakers, and we ourselves are stuck in childhood patterns that wound our partners?

Consciousness is the key; it changes everything. When we are unaware of the unconscious agenda of romantic love, it *is* a disaster because our childhood scenarios inevitably repeat themselves with the same devastating consequences. There is method to this madness, though. The unconscious recreation of the ambiance of childhood has the express purpose of bringing this old impasse to a resolution. When we understand that we have chosen our partners to heal certain wounds and that the healing of those wounds is the key to the end of longing, we have taken the first step on the journey to real love.

Conflict Is Natural

We need to understand and accept that *conflict is supposed to happen.* This is as nature intended it: everything in nature has a polarity and is in tension. The hard truth is that the grounds for marriage really come down to incompatibility; being different is the norm for relationships.

Conflict needs to be understood as a given—a sign that the psyche is trying to survive, to get its needs met and become whole and, paradoxically, to restore connection. It's only without this knowledge that conflict becomes destructive.

The hard truth is that the grounds for marriage really come down to incompatibility; being different is the norm for relationships.

Romantic love is supposed to end. It is the glue that initially bonds two incompatible people together to do what needs to be done to heal each other and, in the process, heal the rifts in nature caused by our wounds. The good news is that through this process the power struggle also comes to an end. That is, the emotional bond that is created by romantic love to keep partners together through the hard times evolves into a powerful *organic* bond through the process of resolving conflict.

The way we have come to see it is that nature is healing itself in our relationships, restoring connection with split-off parts. This is a spiritual process with psychological benefits. Each individual is a node of energy woven into the tapestry of Being, and the tapestry is frayed and weakened where there is conflict. With self-awareness, we are able to move out of childhood ruts; we are uniquely able to correct what has gone wrong. And when we do, it has cosmic consequences. When we heal our relationships, we heal the rift in nature, repairing the fabric of being and, in a small way, contributing to the wholeness of the human situation.

Making the Choice *for a* Conscious Marriage

A Conscious Marriage is not for the faint-hearted, for it requires reclaiming the lost, repressed parts of ourselves that we were told were dangerous to have and that we unconsciously hate ourselves for having. And it means learning more effective coping mechanisms than the crying or anger or withdrawal that have become so habitual for us, rupturing connection. It means reconnecting through dialogue, stretching to give our partners what they need to heal. This is not easy, but it works.

Regardless of what we may believe, relationships are not born of love but of need; real love is born in relationships. You are already with your dream partner but at the moment he or she is in disguise and, like you, in pain. A Conscious Marriage itself is the therapy you need to restore your sense of aliveness and recover your wholeness and set you on the path of real love and reconnection with the Cosmos, which is your essential nature and destiny.

Thriving, Not Surviving

Karen Blaisure

In a 1997 interview, Maya Angelou spoke on her perseverance in living "[n]ot to survive but to thrive with passion and compassion and humor and style."[1] Thriving with such intensity is compelling and challenging. Love, by demanding our own growth, is one way in which we thrive. In a circular pattern, love brings us its joys of passion, compassion, humor, and style and in turn uses them to transform us by helping us grow.

Passion

Although many people err by attributing to romantic feelings proof that they have chosen their life partner correctly, I believe that

Annette Bening and Warren Beatty

ANNETTE: I think it is true that love brings out the best in us. And that's why we seek it out. That is the way we experience the best of ourselves: by loving somebody else and wanting to be there for them.

—*Redbook,* February 1999

danger also exists if we dismiss outright the importance of feeling passionate about, and with, our partner. The heart's knowledge is not infallible or sufficient but it is necessary. Beyond lust, beyond romance, this mysterious force of passion keeps us connected during the tough times—a lifeline during the storms.

Passion is fueled in many ways, and many have tried to explain how we come to be attracted to our partners and how to sustain that attraction. I believe that friendship and gratitude for that friendship strengthen passion physically and emotionally. I have talked with partners together and separately who have cried at the wonder of finding each other. They describe contentment, deep joy of sharing life with the other, and appreciation for their good fortune. They realize that they have what most people want and marvel at how lucky they are that it has happened to them. Yet these partners are more than lucky in love; they have the beliefs and skills that enhance the quality of their relationships. They resolve to be worthy of the love that is past their understanding, for they cherish what they have in each other.

Compassion

I have had the privilege of seeing couples resurrect their relationship because of the strength of compassion, just as I have seen relationships die because of compassion's fragility. Compassion may demand more than we ever thought possible to give. Compassion transpires when two people look into each other's eyes and both know the depth of the other's imperfections and the beauty of the other's qualities and then choose to commit to one another all over again. As love's thread, compassion weaves us together and allows us to share life's journey with empathy, prompting us to forgive our partner and ourselves when we falter. Both the giving and the receiving of forgiveness and understanding refine us and bind us closer to one another.

Humor

Humor and play are love's enchantments, charming our hearts into a shared rhythm. Daily distractions interrupt our tempo of two, but humor and play unite us for brief bright moments. When I see couples laughing together I think of hope sustained: the hope of understanding, of sharing vulnerabilities, of rescuing a chaotic conversation, of being together tomorrow.

Humor and play are love's enchantments, charming our hearts into a shared rhythm.

During the close times, humor and play are two sure rewards of relationships. During the confusing and tense times, we can rely on them to get us through. Humor rescues us from anger and pride by relaxing us and soothing our emotions. Playing together rescues us from drifting apart, reminding us of our attraction for each other. Sharing humor and play keeps us from being bound too closely to the cares of daily life that all too often steal our energy until little or none is left for those we love. Laughter can readjust our focus and lure us back to our shared rhythm, helping us to live life lightly and with delight.

Style

Love beckons us to know ourselves and to be ourselves. However, the desire to love and to be loved may tempt us to twist ourselves out of recognition. Once we've lived a bit and perhaps twisted a bit, we realize the necessity and perhaps urgency in being ourselves and returning home to our own unique style. We recognize the allure of those who joyfully embrace life and neither hide nor apologize for who they are. We admire and are attracted to such authenticity because it invites, and even expects, the same in us.

Love and authenticity often exist within an abiding and deeply respectful friendship. As friends, we delight in the other "as is," share one another's worlds, and assume responsibility for nurturing the relationship and each other. Some couples with whom I've talked explain that their mutuality and respect for each other's uniqueness serve to "divorce proof" their marriage. It is through honoring uniqueness, paradoxically, that they experience a oneness.

Our hope is to become better versions of ourselves for the commitment to love.

When we enter into a committed relationship, we hope that our lives will become richer emotionally and even spiritually, and that we will thrive. That is, our hope is to become better versions of ourselves for the commitment to love. Love requires us to move beyond our personal fears and limitations and take a simple, yet breathtaking step: to share life's journey with another person. When we choose to do so, we become explorers—of ourselves and one another. And although we are aware that unknown demands may challenge us beyond our comprehension, we commit to a life of discovery with our beloved.

NOTE

1. Taylor, E. "Uncaged: Talking with Maya Angelou About Reading, Writing, and the Temper of the Times." *Chicago Tribune Books Section,* Sept. 28, 1997, p. 3.

What Should Fools Find in Love?

Wyndol Furman

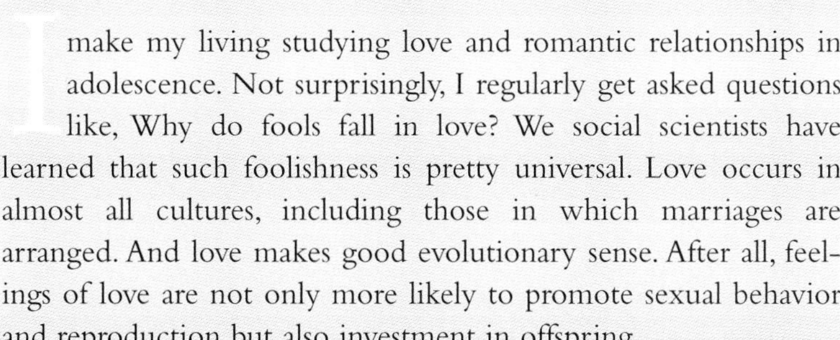

I make my living studying love and romantic relationships in adolescence. Not surprisingly, I regularly get asked questions like, Why do fools fall in love? We social scientists have learned that such foolishness is pretty universal. Love occurs in almost all cultures, including those in which marriages are arranged. And love makes good evolutionary sense. After all, feelings of love are not only more likely to promote sexual behavior and reproduction but also investment in offspring.

A tougher question is why we fall in love with a particular person. We know that proximity, similarity, responsiveness, and sexual and physical attractiveness all seem to matter. Yet that still leaves plenty of people we could fall for out there, doesn't it? Some we fall for and some we don't; it's hard for social scientists to predict who will be attracted to whom. For that matter, it isn't so easy for you to predict either! Numerous variables seem relevant, and they don't combine in any simple way. It makes predicting the weather look easy, and we know how well even the experts can do that!

Consider the first time I met the love of my life. I was two hours late, as I approached her carrying a magnolia branch in an Orange Crush bottle. And what were the magic words that came from my mouth as I handed her that precious glass vessel? "Peace." It was the Sixties. Yet somehow everything clicked, and soon we two fools were madly in love. You'd have been a lot safer predicting that it was going to snow in July than predicting that.

Although there is some mystery about whom we fall in love with, there is less mystery in what makes for a successful, rewarding relationship. In other words, we may not really know why fools fall in love with particular people, but we do have some good ideas about what fools should find in love. Two of the key elements inherent in most successful relationships are a *safe haven* and *a secure base.*

A safe haven is a person you can turn to when you are upset, hurt, sick, or troubled. And being there during those times of distress is when it really matters. It's great that the person is there when things are going well, but you'll do okay if they occasionally are not. But it is important that your partner be there when you're hurting. These are the times when we most need to feel safe turning to our partner for support. It gives you a sense of security—a sense that she or he is there when needed most. And by the same reasoning, it is

Kim Basinger and Alec Baldwin

KIM: It's like, "no matter what comes down, it's you and me, pal, together." He trusts me to the ends of the world, and I trust him. There are no ifs.

—*Ladies Home Journal,* February 1998

important that you are available and responsive when your partner is hurting. It gives him or her a sense of security—a sense that *you* can be trusted, too. Safety and trust can only be achieved when neither partner feels guarded or unsafe.

When you have that sense of safety, you can also develop a secure base from which to explore the world. That is, it is easier to venture out and try new things if you have a safe place or secure base to return to. In a successful relationship, your partner encourages you to develop your interests and talents. It is as if your partner is your number-one fan. When you feel this kind of security, you can flourish and grow without worrying about getting hurt or being in each other's way. In less successful relationships, however, people do not feel supported by their partner and instead feel constrained. Partners often fear rather than support the other's independence. Ironically, though, intimacy and autonomy can go hand in hand. A loving partner permits you to develop yourself, and your own development permits you to grow close to your partner.

One of the paradoxes of relationships is that we are not initially attracted to people on the basis of whether they are good candidates for being a safe haven or a secure base. Those aren't very sexy qualities, are they? I doubt whether we ever will be initially attracted by them. Perhaps we couldn't judge those characteristics accurately even if we wanted to; we need opportunities to see whether someone will be there when we're distressed. We need time to see if someone supports our own individual development, as well as our development as a couple. Some people may naturally be inclined to act as safe havens and secure bases, but others may need to learn how to do that with you. You yourself may also need practice, and the two of you may need to work on this as a pair. Whether a secure base evolves naturally or emerges through hard work, I'd want to see evidence of these traits before I made a lasting commitment.

Mind you, relationships can be fun and rewarding even without having a safe haven or secure base. My research with hundreds of teenage relationships reveals that most of them don't fully have these features. And that's not surprising. Adolescence is a time of experimenting and learning about romantic relationships. For that matter, many casual *adult* relationships focus on fun and companionship rather than on safety and security, and they too are rewarding. But if you're talking about a committed relationship—a long-term relationship—then these two features should certainly be central.

If I were looking for a relationship now, I'd probably . . . bring flowers . . . be a bit more articulate . . . and I might even try to be on time.

We may never be able to predict who is attracted to whom and why. Who would ever have guessed that my future wife would be attracted to a hippie holding an Orange Crush bottle? If I were looking for a relationship now, I'd probably put that bottle aside and spare the magnolia tree. I might bring flowers though. I'd try to be a bit more articulate, and I might even try to be on time.

My behavior would undoubtedly be different, but I'd still be seeking that initial attraction and excitement, no matter how old I was. After all, the fireworks and passion of the early phases are great fun.

What then should fools find in love? Many things, certainly. But if what I most wanted was a wonderful and enduring lifetime partner, I'd try to develop a relationship that provides a safe haven and a secure base for us both. Ultimately, these are the features that make relationships so rewarding.

What's Love Got to Do with It?

Lori Gordon

For one human being to love another, that is perhaps the most difficult of all tasks, the ultimate, the last test and proof, the work for which all other work is but preparations. We must not forget, when we love, that we are beginners, bunglers of life, apprentices in love and must learn love.—Rainer Marie Rilke

He was *the man:* tall, dark, handsome, brilliant smile, dashing; he drove a shiny white convertible; he was successful, self-confident; women swooned. And he wanted me! But then, he was tone deaf, had no skills. In all ways he was self-centered, dictatorial, smug, arrogant, used to being waited on, sulky; he thought sex an assault, children an annoyance; he had weak character; he cheated, flirted. Was he the right person? Definitely not.

He was a magnificent *nature boy*—sexy, sultry, muscular, blue-eyed, bare-footed, a musical genius, played Brahms on the piano; he was a Viking at sea, Adonis in bed, poetic, passionate, romantic. Was he the right one? Impractical, a lost child. I had to figure everything out for him. No, not him. (He wore out his welcome.)

He was every woman's dream—a military *hero;* he was Kevin Costner, wore the uniform, the colors, tipped the cap to perfection; his eyes were a penetrating blue; he was a Leader of men, a Lover of women, strong, insightful, authoritative, gentle, eloquent, knowledgeable, romantic; we had superb chemistry. Was he the right one? Maybe. Maybe not. The timing was off. He was entangled. Too much pretense, too many lies, too good to be true. He wasn't true. Forget him. (It was hard to do.)

He was confident, accomplished, curious, kind, funny, patient, persevering, learned, and playful. He was musical (sang harmony to my melody), athletic (we could play tennis, table tennis; we could bike ride, swim together), romantic, imaginative, sentimental, poetic, thoughtful, empathic, and affectionate, wonderful dancer, effective, intelligent, exploring, curious. We talked a lot, laughed a lot. He encouraged me, appreciated me. He was proud of me, open, accepting; he was interested in and kind to my children. Was he the right one? Oh yes!

What Makes for the Right One

What makes for the right one? Humor, confidence, mutual respect, empathy, kindness, character, interest, confiding, listening, friendship, patience, chemistry, companionship, mutual trust. And *timing* is important. If either one of you appears at the wrong time, it doesn't work.

We could love and trust each other. He freed me to spend time and energy, to be productive in my work instead of worrying about the state of our relationship. He was constant, loving, generous, spiritual, encouraging, accepting. He didn't hold grudges.

I could work late, return home later than he or I had planned, and he would rise to greet me with a welcoming hug. He respected that indeed if I was late, there were valid reasons, and he was happy to see me when I arrived. He trusted that it wasn't a move I made against him. No grudges. We would sit down and debrief the day's events, have a meal, watch the news, curl up in bed in each other's arms, and sleep.

The Journey

The journey was anything but smooth. I first married at nineteen at the end of my sophomore year at college. We had known each other less than three months. I found that nothing of what I'd learned about love came to be. The marriage lasted seventeen years. It did not fare well. I returned to graduate school, thinking that there I would find the answers to the puzzle of intimate relationships, what nurtured them and what sabotaged them. I didn't find the answers. I came to realize that the skills my husband had learned in law school served him well in his career. But he knew nothing of intimacy, of confiding, of affection, of constancy. And he didn't want to know.

I set out to find answers to the question of how to sustain love in intimate relationships. I did not ever want to endure again what I had in this marriage, either for myself or for my children.

The journey led me to people and experiences that taught me important life lessons—lessons that aren't taught in graduate school or in the media.

I found that a truly good relationship is healing emotionally, spiritually, and physically. It is a source of growth and creativity.

I found that a truly good relationship is healing emotionally, spiritually, and physically. It can be an ecstatic and spiritual experience. It is a source of growth and creativity. A miserable relationship is a source of depression, illness, rigidity, and a complete range of acting out behaviors, for both children and adults.

The heart of intimacy is bonding, sharing emotions, and being able to confide in a loving partner who wants to know you, who can empathize, and who is capable of a range of physical closeness, from affection, comfort, and tenderness through sensuality and sexuality. I know now that these things are not expendable, that they can come at any point in your life if you value them enough to wait, and that they can assume many shapes and sizes in another person.

Barometers of a Relationship

I like to think of the lessons I learned as *Barometers of a Relationship.* After many false starts and years of learning, I'm now very happy. Let me tell you what I've discovered, both in my own life and from working with thousands of couples:

- *Commitment:* Each person must be capable of sustaining mutual trust, honesty, and fidelity and of nurturing a relationship. Commitment means you trust each other to go the distance.

- *Self-worth:* When self-worth or confidence is low, it is easy to misperceive and misread what is happening with significant others and to react in negative, destructive ways. Positive self-esteem is so important to being able to reveal ourselves, confide, trust, and allow ourselves to be known to each other.

- *Communication:* The emotional bond of confiding in each other, friendship, openness, empathy, and compassion—this is

Will Smith and Jada Pinkett

WILL: She's just someone with whom I can talk to about anything. I've never been able to step outside of my maleness to share myself with someone. She's the first person with whom I was able to break that down.

—*Ebony,* September, 1997

the heart of intimacy. Without that bond, love as an emotion withers. It is so easy to misunderstand, to miscommunicate. For people who don't express themselves naturally or easily, *the good news is that communication can be learned.*

- *Chemistry:* A unique physical magnetism for each other seems to be irreplaceable. Although sexual technique can be learned, pheromones are a natural substance that fuel attraction and are not manufactured. When the magnetism has been there, it can be restored, if obstacles in the relationship that have interfered can be removed. However, if the physical magnetism has never been there, good sexual technique will not replace it. Nor can technique replace the magnetic pleasure of hands and lips naturally reaching out and touching, bodies melting into each other, and the aroma that only your partner's body offers.

  There are different levels of physical attraction. At different life periods, its importance and urgency in the relationship varies. I have found one thing certain: an unhappy relationship will overwhelm pleasure and can destroy physical closeness. When other forms of closeness and emotional bonding are not present, the physical attraction can easily disappear.

- *Humor:* It is so important to be able to laugh together, to play together, to ride the pony (have the pleasure), not just clean the barn (do the work). Humor is one of our most sensitive barometers. When the other elements of a relationship are diminished, so are humor and laughter.

- *Building together:* Time and life grow us and change us. All of the above will not sustain love if we're not willing to grow and change together. We want our partner as our best friend. As we acquire ties, children, home, family, community, and careers we need to continue to share values, interests, mutual trust, mutual respect, companionship, and a mutual willingness to go the distance.

Each of us needs to be personally ready to do that. And capable. And we need the skills.

10 Traits of Love

Amy K. Olson and David H. Olson

Although we have researched couples and families extensively, we have no precise definition of love. In fact, because of its complexity, scientists often ignore love. Love is a powerful agent in human behavior and usually the foundation of marriage, yet it continues to be elusive and defy definition. To define love it seems would be to also reduce its significance and magnitude. Nevertheless, we offer the following 10 Traits of Love with the hope that they will help couples increase their understanding and mastery over this powerful but elusive agent.

1. ***Love is a magical process that creates couple chemistry***. Like a chemical reaction, love creates a new entity when two people are

> But love is blind and lovers cannot see
> The petty folies that themselves commit.
>
> —William Shakespeare, *The Merchant of Venice*

in love. The whole is also greater and different from the sum of the parts. In chemistry, 2 molecules of hydrogen and 1 molecule of oxygen (H_2O) create water. So it is with couples. If one of the partners in a couple should pair with a different person (like a different element in chemistry), the resulting product would be different.

2. *Love is often blind.* Love impairs our vision so we see the world through rose-colored glasses. Love causes us to see things more optimistically than they actually are, which interferes with our knowledge and true discovery of each other. For this reason, family and friends often know who is a better long-term match for you than you do for yourself. People outside an intimate relationship have a different perspective—one that enables them to see things you may not be able to see because you are too emotionally close. An analogy can be drawn to how we view our environment. If you were in Italy, standing inches away from the leaning tower of Pisa, it would appear straight because of how close you were to it. If you stood back far enough to see the whole tower, however, you would see that the tower actually leans quite dramatically.

3. *Love changes over time.* The beginning stages of love are typically very romantic and idealistic. Over time, love slowly becomes less idealistic and more realistic. Some of the excitement that comes from the mystery and newness of another person will inevitably dissipate with discovery. But real love will continue to grow and mature in deeper and more meaningful ways as you nurture it and keep it alive.

4. *Love-based marriages are more fragile than arranged marriages.* Because the nature of love is always changing, a couple in a love-match marriage may feel threatened by the natural changes of love. They may interpret the change as "falling out of love" and may think about getting out of the relationship. And although love is an important ingredient in marriage, it should not be the only one.

We know that in the United States where love-match marriages occur, the divorce rate continues to be about 40 to 50 percent. During the early stages of a relationship, it probably appears to both individuals that love is all they need to get them through any circumstance. And although newlyweds are by nature idealistic, at some point reality sets in and issues such as fairness, respect, equality, and emotional compatibility become more important. Whether love will prevail will be determined by the quality of the relationship and each partner's commitment to it.

5. *Superficial love fades over time.* With superficial love, the best and most intense moments are at the beginning of the relationship—the stage of "falling in love." This kind of love tends to be equated with sex, attraction, security, and romance. As reality inevitably dissolves this type of unstable love, the relationship becomes progressively less satisfying. Superficial love may feel intense, but it is really a delicate phenomenon.

6. ***Real love grows over time.*** With real love, the positive feelings don't diminish with time. Couples experiencing real love will often express that they love their partner increasingly over time. Real love enables both individuals to grow. Real love does not just happen but is the result of the process of committing yourself to the relationship.

7. ***Our language of love is inadequate.*** We are limited by the language we have to describe love. Love is much more complex than what we often express. The word *love* is often used too loosely in our culture. Can we possibly be expressing the same thoughts and emotions when we say, "I love pizza," "I love football," and "I love you"? Similarly, although Eskimos have many different words to describe what we simply call snow, we basically have one word to describe love. How then do we describe love when love is infinite and beyond definition?

In order to experience love, you must be vulnerable to it.

8. ***Love is often misdiagnosed.*** Related to the language barriers in describing love is the common misdiagnosis of love. People often make the mistake of using the word *love* when what they really are describing is passion, excitement, enjoyment, or need.

9. ***Love is paradoxical.*** Love endures. Love fades. Love is both limited and unlimited. Love can conquer anything, yet we often feel conquered by it. In marriage and couple relationships, love helps get the relationship off to a good start because it energizes

the couple to connect. But it is not sufficient for a lasting relationship. Unless couples have and use good relationship skills to protect their love, it will fade over time.

10. ***Giving love is receiving love.*** When love is given away, it remains with you as well. In fact, love is unique in that the more you give, the more you will have to give and the more you will undoubtedly receive. There is an unlimited supply of love within each of us. All we need to do is open ourselves to it and then give it away. In order to experience love, you must be vulnerable to it. Creating emotional barriers with the intention of protecting yourself from hurt only restricts and limits the flow of love into your life.

You cannot truly give love without receiving love. Giving love away increases rather than depletes love. Love is magical and paradoxical. Although love is necessary for intimacy, it is not sufficient for maintaining an intimate relationship over time. Hence the paradox of love.

Who Took My Prince?

Sunny Shulkin

As my husband, Mark, and I toast each other for forty-five years of marriage, I marvel. Given our rocky journey, how could we have made it? I'm in awe of the courage it takes for two people to *remain* in a committed relationship when the path to happiness is both unclear and daunting. *Entering* a relationship requires something else: putting on rose-colored glasses. How difficult could it be to fall in love? Not very. Even teenagers do it.

Putting on Rose-Colored Glasses

In the beginning, love is easy. You're my prince and I'm your princess. We shrug off anyone who hints that our glasses are a bit clouded. Such cynics! But here's what happens:

❧ *Chemistry keeps our lenses rose colored (for a while).* The chemist stands in his laboratory, pouring contents from one test tube into another. He glances up as I enter and says, "So, you see a prince. But do you know it's his smell that draws you in? His DNA is embedded in each of his sweat glands and that's what you smell!" he says. "Ha!" I laugh. He continues. "You are meant to be attracted to someone whose DNA is incompatible with yours. There's a better chance of healthy offspring. This prince of yours just has the right DNA!" This chemist is relentless. "So once you two come together, what gets you to the altar? More drugs. Endorphins for a sense of well-being. Adrenaline for the rush. Oxytocin for bonding and, for a final touch, phenoethelamine—PEA for short. It's responsible for your libido spike! But drugs don't last forever, sweetheart. What then? Will he still be a prince?" I pretend to ignore him, but moisture forms around my rose-colored glasses.

❧ *Psychology keeps our lenses rose colored (for a while).* The psychologist enters, smoking his pipe and stroking his salt-and-pepper-colored beard. "Do you realize your attraction is due to your unconscious agenda to find someone who will meet your unmet childhood needs? Come the wedding bells and you'll discover he is as incapable of meeting your needs as were your parents. What will you do? You'll begin to relate to one another through your defenses. You'll criticize; he'll withdraw. Need I say more?" "Enough," I say. "You don't know him like I know him.

He's not at all like my mother or my father. He meets all my needs. It's not a problem." I tuck away the recent shock of my partner's being upset over my driving—shades of my critical father. He must have had a bad day.

Christopher Reeve and Dana Morosine

CHRISTOPHER: The most important thing is the fact that Dana still feels the same way about me as she did when we first met. I go forward because of the love I have in our own family.

—*Redbook,* February 1999

Sociology keeps our lenses roses colored (for a while). "I want to put a word in here," says the sociologist, going through her research. "Your culture supports different functions, depending on your gender or your culture's expectations. Let's suppose that in your family—the transmitter of your culture—girls think and feel but aren't sexual or acknowledged for bold achievement. In such a case, you'll feel whole and alive around a partner who has those missing functions."

"What's the problem?" I ask cautiously. She replies, "When your rose-colored glasses slip, you'll be frustrated by the very qualities that you now admire. You'll go back to the partial self that feels more like you. After all, your old brain stores archaic memories of whether you were accepted or rejected for being whole. If the answer comes back, 'Accepted? No way!' you'll reject those aspects of him that were forbidden in you. You'll try and get him to be more like you, but he's in a similar fix." I shove my glasses back on and slip out.

- ***Physics keeps our lenses rose colored (for a while).*** She looks like Albert Einstein, with her nose to the chalkboard. Her mind is filled with various formulas and energy models. Sensing my presence, she speaks. "Ah," she says, staring at my tinted lenses, "You're at the beginning of your relationship. No doubt you like his energy, yes? He is the calm, collected one, yes?" I nod. "Ah," she plows on, "You must be the emotional one who can fill the spaces with enthusiasm and verve, yes?" I nod. "Who wants to tell you that a year from today you'll feel lonely around his self-sufficient ways and he'll feel overwhelmed by your needs and feelings. Not me." As I close the door behind me, I notice that she too wears glasses. Why are hers so clear?

It takes courage to remove rose-colored lenses and face relationships wearing clear ones. Only then do you know the person, your partner, not the illusion. What do you need to do to clarify those lenses? Here are five steps you can take:

Cleansing the Lens #1: *Expect and Embrace Incompatibility*

In every relationship that moves beyond the stage of romantic love, there is difference. When we see the differing other, whose reality is miles apart from our own, we're shocked. Finding ourselves with someone who thwarts us rather than supports us was not part of the bargain. Our glasses darken with frustration.

> If we live together before marriage, won't we find out if we're incompatible? No. Incompatibility shows up after the commitment, not before.

My husband, Mark, had repeated abandonment experiences in childhood. My childhood was marked by invasiveness. He championed closeness and I preferred separation. We struggled. With such differing histories and differing strong suits, we tried on the possibility that we had something to learn from one another. He could teach me about togetherness that didn't suffocate, and I could teach him about separation without the sting of loneliness.

Cleansing Solution #1: Accept difference as essential for your growth.

Cleansing the Lens #2: *Become a Source of Safety*

We all want to feel safe in our intimate relationship. In romantic love, it was our prince who created it and now that it's missing, we wait for him to restore it. As powerless children, we waited for someone else to make life safe for us. We wait again. Paradoxically, when we stop waiting and become a source of safety for the other, we ourselves feel safe and empowered.

Cleansing Solution #2: Find out what makes your partner feel safe around you. Try it on.

Cleansing the Lens #3: *Become a Source of Aliveness*

It's wonderful when safety is restored, but we want more. With safety alone, our energy becomes stale, routine, fixed. We need aliveness, too. PEA is restored in the context of adventure, surprise, freshness, risk, and novelty. Paradoxically, to the extent that we become a source of aliveness for our partner, we activate our own aliveness.

Cleansing Solution #3: Discover what aliveness means to your partner. Move in that direction.

Cleansing the Lens #4: *Gift Your Partner*

We will ask things of our partners that seem unappealing to them. They may want a fuss made over their birthday. We hate fuss. We ask for affection in public from someone who squirms at the thought. When we can view our partner's requests as an opportunity for us to experience life freely, it will open up our own suppressed territory. Ultimately, gifting our partner helps us grow. It gives us the opportunity for mastery in the exact areas in which we need to mature, as well as with insight into childhood interactions that led to our difficulty in the first place.

It's tougher to love a human being than a prince. Unlike princes, human beings are fragile and resilient, wounded and extraordinary, all at the same time. Loving a human being is a sign of your own maturity.

An early request of Mark's was that I tell him something personal about myself. I had become such a workaholic that after a few days, I said, "Mark, I can't think of anything personal about me." He replied, "Sunny, that's personal." Mark's brilliant request led to my own discovery that I had rejected and abandoned much of my personal self in my compulsive drive to achieve. In doing so I had re-created an earlier experience of rejection at the unconscious hands of my hard-working parents. Shortly afterward, I cut back on my schedule and basked in the newness of rest and play. Gifting Mark by honoring his request led to greater abundance of self and relationship for me.

Cleansing Solution #4: Gift your partner's do-able requests. Expect discomfort. It's a sign of growth.

Cleansing the Lens #5: *Find Courage*

It takes courage to find those places in us that won't let love in—or won't offer love unless we're certain we are wanted. None of us can create mature love without a fistful of courage, because reality love requires moving in your partner's direction while maintaining a foundation and a world of your own. It never took courage to love a prince. But it does take courage to love someone who, like all human beings, is both fragile and extraordinary. Love is not and has never been for the weak of heart, even though it's a gift for the soul.

Cleansing Solution #5: Re-image yourself, your partner, and your relationship as courageous. Now accept and offer congratulations for each step either one of you takes along the journey to love!

Unraveling the Mysteries of Love

Howard J. Markman

I think a man and a woman should choose each other for life, for the simple reason that a long life with all its accidents is barely enough for a man and a woman to understand each other; and to understand is to love.—William Butler Yeats

"Are great relationships possible?" I am often asked. "You are the relationship wizard . . . the Merlin of Marriage. Do you know any couples who are having great relationships? Please tell me what they are doing right!"

Basically, people want to know: Can I have a great relationship? Can I find a mate who understands and respects me, is nuts about me, treasures and pampers me, will not conquer me and take me for granted, is a happy and content person, and is a great lover, parent, friend, and companion?

This essay and this book were inspired, in part, by these questions. Because I am what you might call a relationship optimist, my answer is, unequivocally, "Yes, we can all find love and happiness" *if* we are able to understand the magical side of love and unravel and master its inherent mysteries.

Why Do Fools Fall in Love?

Love can fuel great deeds—heroic acts and sacrifice; it can bring mental and physical well-being, longer life, happy children, and tremendous personal growth. But love can also fuel negativity and destruction—depression, substance abuse, damaged children—and the erosion of self-esteem. Given these risks, why do we fall in love?

The answer is deceptively simple: we are creatures built for love. We human beings are biologically wired to be attractive and attracted to others. We need to be attached to one other person who accepts us in order to flourish in life, as we work and play. Thus I believe that a long-term, mutually satisfying, committed relationship is the natural state for human beings. And this has been the general human situation across time and across cultures.

Every study I've read reveals that both men and women want more than anything to have a happy, marriage-type relationship. People wish for a special friend who will listen to them, be accepting and understanding, be a companion for the fun times, offer support for the hard times, and be a teammate with whom they can create a vision for the future. We discover this theme in music, literature, poetry, and conversations between friends; we see it in Personal ads on the Internet—wherever there is talk of love. We observe these yearnings from adolescents, young parents, professional couples, empty nesters, senior citizens—everyone.

Once we have experienced love, nothing in life is quite the same, and nothing in life can do what love does.

When we are not in this kind of special, great relationship, even the most happy, content, and secure people tend to be looking for one. In fact, the major complaints of unhappily married men and woman revolve around the lack or loss of the romance, intimacy, and commitment that define a great love.

Toward the Understanding of Love's Mysteries

In my work as a researcher, teacher, and clinician, and in my own life, over the past twenty years, I have learned that there is no greater magic than love. When we are in love we think, act, and feel differently. Once we have experienced love, nothing in life is quite the same, and nothing in life can do what love does.

I've also discovered certain core truths that I hope can guide lovers as they experience the magical mystery tour through the realm of love. These six truths can help us understand love's mysteries.

TRUTH 1: ***What we love the most about our partner can come back to haunt us.***

One of love's greatest mysteries is why the sources of initial attraction and astonishment often are the same sources of disappointment and conflict later on. Research tells us that how we handle these inevitable problems predicts future happiness or divorce.

In general, the early stages of love are fueled by projections, hopes, and wishes. As we get to know our beloved, disappointments and disagreements become inevitable when reality marries fantasy. Yesterday's attraction can become today's complaint or hurt. The same trait that initially seemed appealing—for example, emotional expressiveness or openness—can with time become annoying such as when the person perpetually expresses too much anger. What generally doesn't change is an individual's true nature; what often does change, however, is the generosity with which we view it after repeated hurts.

TRUTH 2: ***When mad, angry, or hurt, it's in your best interest to act counterintuitively.***

A related mystery of love is why, when we are upset, we often instinctively act in ways that turn out to be in opposition to our best interests. Consider how often a spouse who wants more connection and intimacy when angry winds up instead pushing his partner further away. Great lovers are able to act counterintuitively when they are feeling upset: they are able to ascertain what they want to accomplish and rein in impulsive responses that don't serve the best interests of their relationship. Consider that same spouse who now is feeling lonely and, although he desires closeness, doesn't act on these feelings. Instead he allows his partner the space she needs; she recognizes his loving act and bridges the distance in her own way.

TRUTH 3: ***To be the best possible partner, you must be real, centered, confident, personally happy, and content.***

One of the major mysteries of love is why we spend so much of our time and energy looking outward rather than inward. A key to finding and maintaining a great love relationship is to focus on knowing yourself.

Lovers want to be loved and desired for being who they are, not "needed" in order to complete your own unfinished development.

We all have control over our own personal growth and development but very little over our beloved's personality and behaviors. In fact, one of the signs of a relationship headed for trouble is when we assign blame to our partners and focus on changing them rather than ourselves. As many have said, "Love is not about finding the right person but being the right person."

The path to "being the right person" involves being authentic and living fully in the moment. Lovers want to be loved and desired for being who they are, not "needed" in order to complete your own unfinished development. As Hollis noted in an earlier chapter, one of the best gifts you can give your partner is a more developed you.

TRUTH 4: *Don't expect to be your beloved's soul mate before you've been there as your mate's soul unfolds.*

Another mystery of love concerns soul mates. What a wonderful idea—that there exists one person for each of us and if we but find them, true love will blossom and last forever. However appealing this notion may be to our spiritual and romantic sides, I find that soul mates are not created in heaven but evolve here on earth. Too many people focus on deciding whether their partner is "the one" rather than on being the best possible partner they can be with the person they are with.

To be the best lover or soul mate, men and women often need to follow somewhat different paths. For example, men would be wise to focus more on their beloved's feelings, needs, and interests and less on their own desires.

Women may need to understand that although men may seem uncomfortable with conflict and confrontation, they nevertheless want the same things women want: closeness, friendship, and intimacy. Understanding these differences rather than seeking to change them can lead a couple to develop a deeper spiritual bond. In this way, soul mates evolve as lovers grow together and coauthor their own relationship story.

TRUTH 5: ***Invest in your relationship on a daily basis, and resist the temptation to take your partner or relationship for granted.***

One of love's great mysteries is this: Why, when we finally have a great relationship, do we start taking our partner for granted? Doing so often leaves our partner feeling that we just wanted to "conquer" or "win" them. Part of this mystery can be understood as a natural human tendency to respond to the squeaky wheels of life. When things are going well in our relationship we tend to focus our attention and energy elsewhere. Isn't it ironic that we tend to let our lovers know when they upset us, not when they please us?

To counteract these tendencies we must consciously think of treasuring our partners and nourishing our relationships on a daily basis. Send a loving e-mail, give an unexpected hug, say "I love you and appreciate you" (and say why). The more we actively attend to the wonderful aspects of our relationship, the less glaring its problems seem to be.

Men would be wise to focus more on their beloved's feelings, needs, and interests and less on their own desires.

TRUTH 6: ***Love need not be a solitary activity between two people; you need a team of friends to support your journey through a relationship.***

Many of us have the feeling that we're on our own when it comes to enabling our love to survive. The truth is that our relationships can benefit from the support and participation of extended family and friends. In order to make sense of and implement all these core truths, we all might benefit from having our own love or romance team. These are people who not only are our friends—they are *love's* friends. Steer away from people who do not like your beloved or see solely through the eyes of logic and not love. Find people who do not take one side or the other but who side with love and the couple's love interests.

To return to the question I am frequently asked about the possibilities of great relationships: I believe that falling in love and being in love and staying in love are not only possible but easy when our heart is open to it. Love should come naturally, as it did for many of us as children. As adults we are smarter and more in control, yet we often feel that true love is out of reach. We need to connect with our natural, innate potential to love and be loved and let our love grow in a safe and secure vessel, often called marriage. Loving and being loved is essential to personal and societal well-being.

Start with this moment, and as you continue your journey, I hope these six core truths provide a road map to finding and maintaining a great love relationship.

About *the* Authors

JANICE R. LEVINE, Ph.D., is a clinical and developmental psychologist who lives with her husband and two children in Lexington, Massachusetts. Having graduated from Yale and Harvard universities, she is currently clinical instructor in psychiatry at Harvard Medical School's Judge Baker Children's Center.

Levine is coauthor of the book *Fighting* for *Your Jewish Marriage* (Jossey-Bass, 2000) and is the founder-director of the Couples Health Program—a nationally known psychoeducational program that teaches couples how to achieve greater intimacy through communication and the use of conflict resolution skills. She has won many professional honors and awards, appeared in newspapers, magazines, and on TV, hosted her own Parent Education Series, and lectures throughout the United States on various aspects of couples and family relationships.

HOWARD J. MARKMAN, Ph.D., is a leading expert in the couples research and intervention fields. He is professor of psychology at the University of Denver and president of PREP Inc. (Prevention and Relationship Enhancement Program, Inc.). He frequently appears in the national media, including "The Oprah Winfrey Show," "The NBC Today Show," "20/20," and "Nightline" and is invited to speak throughout the United States, Europe, and Australia on the topic of relationships. He is the coauthor of the *Fighting* for *Your*

Marriage Series from Jossey-Bass and coauthor of *The Clinical Handbook of Marriage and Couples Intervention.* He codeveloped PREP and is the author of more than ninety scientific articles and chapters. For information about PREP-related talks and workshops, contact the Web site PREPinc.com, e-mail info@prepinc.com, or call 800-366-0166.

CLAUDIA ARP and DAVID ARP are founders of Marriage Alive, a groundbreaking program that provides training and resources for the church and community. The Arps are popular speakers, seminar leaders, and columnists; they have written numerous books and video curricula, including the award-winning *The Second Half of Marriage* and *10 Great Dates* (Zondervan). They coauthored *Fighting for Your Empty Nest Marriage* with Markman, Stanley, and Blumberg (Jossey-Bass). The Arps are frequent contributors to print and broadcast media; they have appeared as empty nest experts on "The NBC Today Show" and "CBS This Morning." Visit their Web site for more magic marriage tips: www.marriagealive.com. Their e-mail address is TheArps@marriagealive.com.

JESSICA BETHONEY is professor of humanities at Bunker Hill Community College in Boston, where she teaches American culture and cross-cultural studies. She has written for the *Boston Globe* and several other newspapers in the greater Boston area.

KAREN BLAISURE is a licensed marriage and family therapist in Michigan and an associate professor in the Department of Family and Consumer Sciences at Western Michigan University. In addition to her teaching duties, she regularly facilitates couple education classes throughout the state.

RITA M. DEMARIA is renowned for her work in helping couples create loving, stable relationships, even if they are at the brink of divorce. With over twenty-five years of clinical experience, DeMaria is a leading teacher and author in the "marriage movement," teaching PAIRS, PREPARE/ENRICH, and Mars and Venus workshops.

GEORGE DOUB has been a licensed therapist for over thirty years—one of the first Latino therapists in San Jose. He cofounded the Family Wellness Program, founded and directed a crisis counseling program for families in East San Jose, and supervises counselors at a four-thousand-student high school with 85 percent minority students. He consults with schools, industry, and labor on methods to work together more efficiently.

JOHN FISKE has been one of Boston's leading family mediators since 1979, helping couples to divorce or separate gracefully; he now offers mediation to couples who want to renegotiate their marriage and write postmarital agreements.

MARTIE FISKE is an architectural designer, after twenty-eight years of teaching high school English.

PETER FRAENKEL is associate professor of psychology at the City University of New York and director of the Center for Time,

Work and the Family, at the Ackerman Institute for the Family. He is also director of PREP at the NYU Child Study Center. An accomplished jazz drummer, his research is on the rhythms of couple and family life.

WYNDOL FURMAN is professor and director of clinical training in the Department of Psychology at the University of Denver. He has published extensively on adolescent romantic relationships and peer relationships. He and his coauthors, B. Bradford Brown and Candice Feiring, recently edited a book entitled *The Development of Romantic Relationships in Adolescence.*

AMY GERSON is a psychologist in private practice in Lexington, Massachusetts, who treats couples and adults. She provides psychological services and consultation to the New England College of Optometry.

STEPHEN GILLIGAN is a psychologist practicing in Encinitas, California. In addition to his private practice, he travels around the world presenting his work in self-relations psychotherapy to both professional and general audiences. His books include *The Courage to Love, Therapeutic Trances, Brief Therapy* (with J. Zeig), *Therapeutic Conversations* (with R. Price), and *The Legacy of Erickson.* His Web address is www.StephenGilligan.com.

SHIRLEY P. GLASS, a Diplomate in Family Psychology, married her high school sweetheart at age nineteen and received her Ph.D. when her three children were in college. She is the author of *The*

Trauma of Infidelity: Research and Treatment. Her relationship expertise has been featured on the Internet, in the popular press, and on national television. She is in private practice in Baltimore.

LORI GORDON is creator, founder, and president of PAIRS (Practical Application of Intimate Relationship Skills); she lectures and teaches worldwide. She has authored many books, including *Love Knots, Passage to Intimacy, If You Really Loved Me . . .* , and *The PAIRS Program: Preventive Approaches to Couples Therapy* (1999). Gordon teaches emotional literacy through the many PAIRS programs and through PEERS (Practical Exercises Enriching Relationship Skills)—an innovative curriculum for schools.

HENRY GRUNEBAUM is a family therapist who teaches at and runs The Couples and Family Clinic at the Cambridge Hospital, which is associated with the Harvard Medical School. He has a long-standing interest in the subject of romantic love, about which he has learned from his patients and his wife, Judy. He also loves three adult sons, their wives, his four grandchildren, good friends, two dogs, the cello which he plays badly, skiing, and hiking.

W. KIM HALFORD is professor and head of the School of Applied Psychology at Griffith University in Brisbane, Australia. He researches the influences on couple relationships and the effects of relationship enhancement and therapy programs. Halford has published three books and more than eighty research articles on couple relationships; with colleagues, he developed Couple Commitment and Relationship Enhancement (Couple CARE)—a self-directed relationship education program. He maintains an active practice as a couples therapist and relationship educator. Kim is married to Barbara; they have been together for twenty-five years and have two sons, James and Christopher.

HARVILLE HENDRIX cofounded with his wife, Helen L. Hunt, the Institute for Imago Relationship Therapy, which teaches a marital therapy they created. *Getting the Love You Want: A Guide for Couples, Keeping the Love You Find: A Personal Guide,* and *Giving the Love That Heals: A Guide for Parents,* coauthored with Helen, are best-sellers and have been translated into thirty-five languages. Imago Relationship Therapy is taught in eleven countries and has had extensive media coverage, including ten hours on "The Oprah Winfrey Show." For further information call 800-729-1121 or consult www.imagotherapy.com.

JAMES HOLLIS is a Zurich-trained Jungian analyst practicing in Houston, Texas, where he is also executive director of the Jung Educational Center. He is the author of eight books exploring the nexes of psyche and soul, including *The Eden Project: In Search of the Magical Other.*

ART LINKLETTER—a television and radio star for more than sixty years—has performed in two of the longest-running shows in broadcast history: "House Party" and "People Are Funny." His book *Kids Say the Darndest Things* was one of the top fourteen best-sellers in American publishing history. Linkletter has won two Emmy awards and four Emmy nominations, a Grammy award, and has been given ten honorary doctorate degrees; he has written twenty-three books. The honor in which he takes particular pride, however, is having been named Grandfather of the Year in 1962.

PATRICIA LOVE is an educator, speaker, and relationship consultant from Austin, Texas. She is a licensed marriage and family therapist, professional counselor, and past president of the International Association for Marriage and Family Counselors. She lectures internationally, is highly sought after as a guest speaker, and appears regularly on "The Oprah Winfrey Show." Patricia has written three books, including *The Satisfied Heart* and *Hot Monogamy.*

AMY K. OLSON is a research associate at Life Innovations in Minneapolis, Minnesota. She is coauthor of two books, *Empowering Couples: Building on Your Strengths* (2000) and *Building Relationships: Developing Skills for Life* (1999), as well as several professional articles.

DAVID H. OLSON is professor of family social science at the University of Minnesota, St. Paul, and president of Life Innovations. He is primary developer of the PREPARE/ENRICH Program for Couples. He is past president of the National Council on Family Relations (NCFR) and a fellow and clinical member in the American Association of Marital and Family Therapy (AAMFT). He has written over twenty books and one hundred articles in the field of marriage and family. His most recent books include

Marriage and the Family: Diversity and Strengths, third edition (2000) and *Empowering Couples: Building on Your Strengths* (2000).

STEVEN PINKER has served on the faculties of Harvard and Stanford universities; he is currently professor of psychology at MIT. His research on visual cognition and the psychology of language received awards from the National Academy of Sciences and the American Psychological Association. Pinker has written five books, including *The Language Instinct, How the Mind Works,* and *Words and Rules.* He writes frequently for the popular press, including *Time,* the *New York Times,* and *Slate.*

FRANK PITTMAN III, from Atlanta, is a psychiatrist, family therapist, noted international lecturer, prolific writer, film critic for *The Family Therapy Networker,* and former columnist for *Psychology Today* and *New Woman.* He has been in full-time private practice for the last twenty-eight years. His four books are *Turning Points: Treating Families in Transition and Crisis; Private Lies: Infidelity and the Betrayal of Intimacy; Man Enough: Fathers, Sons and the Search for Masculinity;* and *Grow Up! How Taking Responsibility Can Make You a Happy Adult.*

SUNNY SHULKIN is a master trainer in Imago relationship therapy. From her hometown of Bala Cynwyd, Pennsylvania, she leads workshops for couples and training for therapists with her husband Mark Shulkin, and daughter, Nedra Fetterman. Their Web address is www.mentoringlove.com.

Gary Smalley is one of the country's best-known authors and speakers on family relationships. He has authored sixteen best-selling, award-winning books, along with several popular films and videos. His award-winning infomercial, "Keys to Loving Relationships," has appeared to television audiences all over the world. Smalley has appeared on national television programs such as "The Oprah Winfrey Show," "Larry King Live," "The NBC Today Show," and "Sally Jessy Raphael."

Greg Smalley is director of clinical research and development at Smalley Relationship Center and president of Today's Family, a nonprofit counseling center in Branson, Missouri. He has written over seventy articles on parenting and relationship issues and is coauthor of *Bound by Honor, Winning Your Wife Back,* and *Winning Your Husband Back.*

Michael Smalley is the director of media services at Smalley Relationship Center and maintains a counseling practice in Branson, Missouri. He is a frequent guest on radio and TV and lectures extensively on topics related to marriage and family relationships.

Wayne M. Sotile and **Mary O. Sotile** have published five books, including *Beat Stress Together: The BEST Way to a Passionate Marriage, a Healthy Family, and a Productive Life* (Wiley, 1999) and *The Medical Marriage: Sustaining Healthy Relationships for Physicians and Their Families* (American Medical Association, 2000). Frequently featured in the international media, the Sotiles are among today's most sought-after keynote speakers and consultants. They practice what they preach in Winston-Salem, North Carolina.

STEVEN STOSNY, director of CompassionPower, became interested in the healing power of compassion during his childhood in a violent home. He is the author of books, articles, and tapes on the subject, including *The Miracle of Empowered Love.* His groundbreaking work in emotional regulation, described in his *Treating Attachment Abuse,* is practiced worldwide.

SCOTT M. STANLEY is codirector of the Center for Marital and Family Studies at the University of Denver and an adjunct professor of psychology. He is an expert in research on marital commitment. He authored *The Heart of Commitment* (1998) and coauthored the Jossey-Bass best-seller, *Fighting* for *Your Marriage* (1994). In addition, he has authored many professional journal articles, book chapters, and magazine articles, and he regularly comments on marriage for publication in the media.

PEGGY VAUGHAN and JAMES VAUGHAN have written seven books, including *Making Love Stay, The Monogamy Myth,* and *Life-Design.* Since 1996 they have made their work available through their Web site: www.dearpeggy.com. The Vaughans have been married forty-five years and make their home in La Jolla, California.

CHARLIE VERGE is director of the Couple Therapy Training Program, Family Institute of Cambridge. He is a former lecturer in psychiatry at the Harvard Medical School (1984–1994) and codirector of the Family Therapy Training Program at the Massachusetts School of Professional Psychology (1979–1994). Verge offers workshops, retreats, and development groups in spiritually centered psychotherapy from his practice in Newton, Massachusetts.

EMILY B. VISHER is a psychologist in private practice for twenty-eight years. She is currently an adjunct faculty member at John F. Kennedy University, Contra Costa County, California.

JOHN S. VISHER (a medical doctor) was associated with the San Mateo County Community Mental Health Program from 1969 to 1986 and is now lecturer emeritus, Stanford University. Together they have specialized for twenty-five years in working with stepfamilies. In 1979 they were cofounders of Stepfamily Association of America, now based in Lincoln, Nebraska. They have jointly written many professional papers and four books, including *Old Loyalties, New Ties: Therapeutic Strategies with Stepfamilies* and *How to Win as a Stepfamily*. They have given over three hundred presentations and professional stepfamily training workshops in the United States and abroad.

DEE WATTS-JONES, also known as THANDIWE, is a clinical psychologist, family therapist, and poet. She is on the faculty of the Ackerman Institute for the Family and the Family Institute of

Westchester, New York. She has published several professional articles on cultural issues that are related to families of African descent, and her poetry has appeared in *Essence* magazine on several occasions under her thandiwe name, which means "loving one" in Xhosa. She is also a student of the spiritual practices of Buddhism, Ifa, Taoism, and of the Native American people.

Invitation to
Our Readers

Dear Readers,

It's been our pleasure to offer you this compendium of essays about love. This volume was written by the "experts." But it is our belief that we are all equally experts and students alike, and have much to learn from one another about love's magic, mystery, and meaning.

If you have some thoughts that might add to our understanding of love's dimensions, we invite you to submit an essay of 1000 words to be considered for inclusion in our next book. Please send three copies of your essay, along with a 50 word biographical sketch and your mailing address, to: Essay Submission, c/o Janice R. Levine, Ph.D., 76 Bedford St. Suite 19, Lexington, MA 02420, or email it to us directly at: FoolsForLove@aol.com. We will notify you if your essay is selected.

To order books and for more information, please visit our Web site at: foolsforlove.com.

Janice R. Levine ❧ *Howard J. Markman*